Stew Leonard's
WINNING RECIPES
COOKBOOK

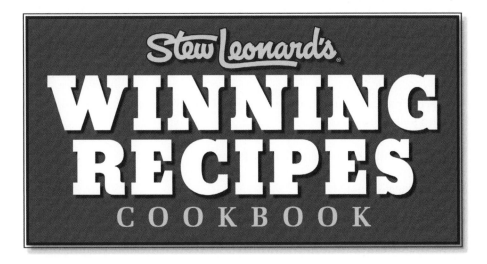

Stew Leonard's
WINNING RECIPES
COOKBOOK

OVER 300 QUICK & EASY RECIPES

Kimberly Press
Norwalk, CT

Kimberly Press and Stew Leonard's are registered trademarks of Stew Leonard's, Inc.

Visit our website at www.stewleonards.com

ISBN 0-96686-11-2-4

Printed in the United States of America
10   9   8   7   6   5   4   3   2   1   hardcover

Book design by Leanne Coppola

Food styling by Anne Egan and Diane Vezza

Food photographs by Lisa Koenig

Store photographs by Richard Lung and Blake Leonard

Illustrations by Soran Kareem

Front cover recipe: Filet Mignon with Wild Mushroom Sauce (page 134)
Back cover recipe: Turkey Scaloppine with Tomatoes and Olives (page 217)

CONTENTS

ACKNOWLEDGEMENTS

Thank you to my mom and dad who had me gather more than 20 people for a tasting to improve our meatballs. They are passionate!

Thank you to the great chefs in New York, Connecticut, Italy, France, and Spain who have shared some of their tips and secrets.

Thank you to our customers. From all the great suggestions you give us every day for how we can serve you better, to the terrific recipes you submitted for our first-ever Customer Recipe Cook-Off, to the fresh ideas you give us in our customer focus groups, your feedback makes us better. We hope you can see your ideas sprinkled throughout the following pages, just like a finely seasoned recipe.

Stew's mom and dad—Marianne and Stew, Sr.

To my entire family, especially my beautiful wife and four daughters—Kim, Blake, Alexandra, Chase, and Madison—thanks for being eager taste testers. To my mom, Marianne, and my dad, Stew, thanks for starting it all and supporting us as we continue to grow. And to my sisters, Beth and Jill, and brother, Tom, our hearts and souls are in our stores and this book, and I look forward to passing our love of food and family on to the next generation of Leonards with you.

I am grateful to the 2,000 Team Members in our stores, whose smiling faces greet and serve our customers daily, especially a few in particular who worked enthusiastically to bring you this book, including Meghan Flynn, Jill Greenwood, Richard Lung, Zita Sebastian, Rich Beladino, Jerry Martellaro, Doreen Miner, Executive Chef George Llorens, and chefs Jackie Lim, Pierre Philitas, Chaz Fable, Chris Angione, Art Weiss, Mike Olbrys, Armand Vanderstiychel, Bob Minnucci, and Chien-Wen Pan.

Thanks to the gang at Sage Communications, especially Anne Egan, who took our recipes and concepts and turned them into this exciting book, and Jennifer Bright Reich, Donna Bellis, Leslie Keefe, Dale Mack, and Nanette Bendyna.

WHY WRITE ANOTHER COOKBOOK?

As the father of four daughters and the husband of a busy wife, I often get a call in the late afternoon from my wife, Kim, who says, "I'm running late; can you bring home dinner?" I have to figure out what I can pick up at our food store and prepare quickly at home so that we can all enjoy dinner as a family.

Because I am in the food business, I also want to make each meal a winner and a WOW. This means using only the best quality, freshest ingredients and needing quick, easy, and delicious recipes that will get the "thumbs up" from my family at the dinner table.

Stew and his family—Chase, wife Kim, Alexandra, Madison, and Blake.

As I walk through the store, I find our customers all in the same predicament. In planning this cookbook, I asked our chefs if they could take our most popular fresh foods and create more than 300 family friendly recipes that are fast to make. The dishes feature the items that Stew Leonard's is known for, such as our milk that arrives daily from our own dairy farm, the artisan breads baked fresh every morning, the just-picked produce harvested from local farms, beef from our Midwest ranchers, fish fresh from the piers, and poultry from Shenandoah Valley and Amish country.

Stew at our dairy farm in Ellington, Connecticut.

Once we selected the best recipes, our team took it a step further. We listened to you, our customers, to determine what your absolute favorites are. They're the foods that you are always asking for suggestions about, for preparing mouthwatering main dishes such as filet mignon, making standard fare like mashed potatoes more exciting, and jazzing up healthy favorites like strawberries. For each of these top foods, we give you not one, not two, but 10 terrific recipes! Look

Chef George judges recipes at our first-ever customer recipe cook-off.

for them in the "10 Winning Ways to WOW" sections of this book.

In addition to more than 300 recipes, we've included hundreds of tips and tricks to streamline food shopping, storing, and cooking. (Look for the shopping 🐷, storing 🗄️, and cooking 🍳 tips included throughout the book.) Also in the book, look for recipes that can be prepared in 30 minutes or less ⏱️ and recipes that are great on the grill 🍖.

You'll also find the top 10 recipes from our recent customer recipe cook-off. These winning recipes were chosen from hundreds of our customers' favorite recipes.

Rich, Tony, and Stew touring vineyards in Tuscany.

A few years ago, Stew Leonard's decided to branch out into the wine business. It made perfect sense; wine is after all most often served with food. I believe so strongly that wine is an essential part of a fabulous meal that for each of the main dishes in this book, our wine experts have recommended a wine pairing. (Look for them next to the wine-pairing symbols 🍷.)

I share my love of food and cooking in each of the following pages, and I hope it inspires you, too! Enjoy!

Stew

THE STEW LEONARD'S STORY

Our story actually began more than 100 years ago.

Samuel "S.J." Stewart—my great-grandfather—opened the first family dairy store in the 1890s on 7th Avenue in Brooklyn, where he sold milk and butter from his dairy farm in Bellevale, New York. He would get the fresh dairy products from the farm in the morning, sell them that day, and then start all over again the next day. It was fresh every day. In the early 1900s, S.J. became interested in the new field of milk pasteurization, and in 1920 he founded the Norwalk Dairy Company, a modern pasteurizing and bottling plant.

My great-grandfather, Samuel Stewart

My grandfather, Charles Leo Leonard

One of S.J.'s first employees was his son-in-law Charles Leo Leonard, who started his own dairy in 1921. Every morning, Charles would get up at 3 a.m., drive by horse and buggy to the farms to get milk, return to the dairy, bottle the milk, then deliver it to his customers.

Charles's son, Stew Leonard, Sr., my dad, joined the family business in 1951. By 1967, my dad realized that the home delivery milk business was "going the way of the iceman." My dad dreamed of opening up a dairy store where customers could watch their

My mom, Marianne, enjoys a glass of milk right from their own dairy.

My dad in his milkman delivery days.

milk being bottled, do their shopping, and have fun. In 1969, my dad wanted to create a store with the same philosophy. With the help of my mom, Marianne, my dad opened a store in Norwalk, Connecticut, with eight items for sale and seven employees. By the end of that year, 10,000 customers were visiting the store each week.

Opening day of Stew Leonard's in December 1969, Norwalk, Connecticut. It was my dad's dream come true.

Over the years, our family's fresh dairy concept expanded to include meats, fish, cheese, produce, freshly baked goods, and wine. The original store in Norwalk has been expanded 35 times to keep pace with its growth.

After 35 additions, the Norwalk store expanded to more than 110,000 square feet.

Today shopping at Stew Leonard's is still a fun-filled, unique experience. Customers are greeted in the store by a costumed cow named Wow and entertained by the Farm Fresh Five—singing milk cartons that perform more than 50,000 times a year. Customers can tour the world's only in-store milk-processing plant at our Norwalk store, where each year more than 10 million half-gallon cartons of milk are packaged from our dairy farm. Plenty of free samples are offered in every department. And always, there's farm fresh food galore.

Cynthia the Chick, WOW the Cow, and Daphne the Duck entertaining shoppers and their children.

Rich and Skim Milk, lead singers in the Farm Fresh Five show.

Because of our country fair atmosphere, Stew Leonard's has been dubbed the "Disneyland of dairy stores" by the *New York Times*. *Ripley's Believe It or Not* featured Stew Leonard's as the "world's largest dairy store," and in 1992, Stew Leonard's earned an entry in the *Guinness Book of World Records* for having the greatest sales per unit area of any single food store in the United States.

We like to describe Stew Leonard's as a super farmer's market-a cross between the traditional grocery store and a farmer's market.

Unlike traditional grocery stores that stock 50,000 items, each Stew Leonard's store carries only 2,000 items—each chosen specifically for its freshness, quality, and value. At Stew Leonard's, 80 percent of our prepared foods are made on-site; fish, meat, and produce arrive fresh each day. What's more, we go directly to the source to buy the products that we sell, meaning farmers, fishermen, and ranchers, many of them local. If you see an item on our store shelves, it was probably harvested just days ago.

Meeting with our apple farmer at the beginning of the season.

From the very beginning, our family-owned and operated stores have focused on offering the best-quality farm fresh foods, all delivered with exceptional customer service in a fun atmosphere. We are so passionate

OUR POLICY

RULE 1
THE CUSTOMER IS ALWAYS RIGHT!

RULE 2
IF THE CUSTOMER IS EVER WRONG, REREAD RULE 1.

Stew Leonard

Stew's three-ton policy rock stands proudly at the front of each store.

about customer service, that carved into a three-ton granite rock at each of our store's entrances are two simple rules we live and breathe by: "Rule #1 — The Customer Is Always Right"; Rule #2 — If the Customer Is Ever Wrong, Reread Rule #1."

We also believe that you can't have a great place to shop without first making it a great place work. It is this philosophy that has helped earn Stew Leonard's a place on *Fortune* magazine's "100 Best Companies to Work For" list for the past four years.

A few of the more than 2,000 Team Members at Stew's who are proud to be part of one of America's top companies to work for, ranked by Fortune magazine.

Today Stew Leonard's remains a family business with three locations—Norwalk and Danbury, Connecticut, and Yonkers, New York, with two additional stores planned—one in East Farmingdale, New York, and the other in Orange, Connecticut. Nearly 2,000 Team Members work at Stew Leonard's, more than 300,000 customers visit a Stew Leonard's each week, and our annual sales are close to $300 million.

Food and wine are our passion, and I hope that some passion pours out of every page in this book. Bon appétit!

Meet the Leonard family: Beth, Marianne, Stew Sr., Jill, Tom, and Stew Jr.

STOCKING THE PANTRY

One of the keys to serving great-tasting meals in minutes is to be prepared. Planning the week's meals is a great way to be organized, yet most of us don't know what we will be cooking for dinner until at least 4 p.m. that day. Whipping up a delicious meal with ease is much simpler if you have a well-stocked pantry, so all you need to do is shop for the main ingredients.

The following is a list of ingredients to have on hand to make your dishes flavorful with minimal effort.

BAKING AND BAKERY

- ☐ Baking powder
- ☐ Baking soda
- ☐ Bread crumbs
- ☐ Breads
- ☐ Cooking spray (canola, flavored, and olive oil)
- ☐ Corn starch
- ☐ Cornmeal
- ☐ Flour
- ☐ Honey
- ☐ Salt
- ☐ Sugar (brown, confectioners', and granulated)
- ☐ Vanilla extract

BOXED, CANNED, AND JARRED GOODS

- ☐ Artichoke hearts (marinated)
- ☐ Beans
- ☐ Broth (beef, chicken, and vegetable)
- ☐ Capers
- ☐ Clam juice
- ☐ Clams
- ☐ Marinara sauce
- ☐ Olives
- ☐ Pasta (dried)
- ☐ Pesto
- ☐ Rice
- ☐ Roasted red peppers
- ☐ Sun-dried tomatoes
- ☐ Tomato paste
- ☐ Tomatoes
- ☐ Tuna

Condiments

- ☐ Horseradish
- ☐ Hot sauce
- ☐ Ketchup
- ☐ Maple syrup
- ☐ Mayonnaise
- ☐ Mustard
- ☐ Oil (olive, peanut, and vegetable)
- ☐ Relishes
- ☐ Soy sauce
- ☐ Vinegar (balsamic, red wine, and white wine)

Dairy Staples

- ☐ Butter
- ☐ Cheeses
- ☐ Eggs
- ☐ Half-and-half
- ☐ Milk
- ☐ Sour cream

Herbs and Spices

- ☐ Basil (dried and fresh)
- ☐ Cardamom (ground)
- ☐ Cinnamon (ground)
- ☐ Ginger (ground)
- ☐ Ground red pepper
- ☐ Herbes de Provence
- ☐ Oregano (dried and fresh)
- ☐ Pepper
- ☐ Rosemary (dried and fresh)
- ☐ Rubs for meat and fish
- ☐ Sage (dried and fresh)
- ☐ Thyme (dried and fresh)

Produce

- ☐ Bell peppers (green, red, and yellow)
- ☐ Citrus (lemons, limes, and oranges)
- ☐ Garlic
- ☐ Lettuce
- ☐ Mixed salad greens
- ☐ Nuts
- ☐ Onions
- ☐ Tomatoes

Refrigerated Staples

- ☐ Bacon
- ☐ Caponata
- ☐ Pasta (fresh)
- ☐ Pie crust (frozen)

Miscellaneous

- ☐ Coffee
- ☐ Dried beans
- ☐ Dried fruits
- ☐ Dried grains
- ☐ Wine

APPETIZERS

Appetizers set the stage for a festive gathering. We have included in this chapter some of the most popular appetizers that our chefs serve at the parties they cater, to more everyday appetizers that we sell right in our stores. We also gave you 10 Winning Ways to WOW One-Handed Hors D'oeuvres (page 20) that are easy to make and even more fun to eat. Also, in this chapter, you'll find the secrets behind our refreshing California Guacamole Dip (page 35), zesty Buba's Salsa (page 23), and ever-popular Hot-Selling California Rolls (page 24).

We often serve appetizers on a stick at Stew Leonard's wine tasting events. They are simple to make, a breeze to serve, and easy to eat, especially if you have a wine glass in your other hand. Here you'll find recipes for three of our favorites: Sesame Chicken Saté (page 20), Chef George's Filet on a Stick (page 21), and Chef Mike's Lollipop Chicken (page 22).

Largely because our roots are in the dairy business, cheeses of all varieties are a big favorite at Stew Leonard's. We buy some of our cheeses directly from expert cheese makers, from as varied locations as Europe, New York, Vermont, and Wisconsin. Other cheeses are made right in our stores, such as our fresh mozzarella, which is made by a third generation master mozzarella maker. You'll find several recipes in this chapter include specialty cheeses, such as mozzarella and Parmesan in the Three-Cheese Mini Calzones (page 26), Gorgonzola and blue cheese in the Red Grape Salad (page 31), Saga blue cheese in the Blue Ribbon Blue Cheese Coins (page 32), and smoked Cheddar cheese in the Caramelized Onion Quesadillas (page 38).

I hope you enjoy making and eating these appetizer recipes as much as we enjoyed creating them.

10 Winning Ways to WOW

One-Handed Hors D'oeuvres

It drives me crazy when I am at a party, holding a glass of wine and talking with my friends, and along comes a person with a tray of hors d'oeuvres that requires both hands to eat. I'm a fanatic at our store wine tasting events to have the chefs prepare "one-handed" hors d'oeuvres or appetizers on a stick. Here are 10 of our most popular appetizers that can be eaten as is—no fork needed. When using wooden skewers for grilled or broiled foods, soak them in cold water for 30 minutes before using.

1. SESAME CHICKEN SATÉ: In a small bowl, combine ¼ cup soy sauce, 3 tablespoons rice wine vinegar, 1 tablespoon sesame oil, ½ teaspoon sugar, ¼ teaspoon ground ginger, and ⅛ to ¼ teaspoon red pepper flakes. Place 3 tablespoons of the mixture into a ziptop plastic bag. Add 1½ pounds chicken tenders, about 20. Turn to coat and seal the bag. Refrigerate for 30 minutes to 2 hours. Remove the tenders from the marinade and thread

each onto small skewers, discarding the marinade. Preheat the grill or broiler. Grill or broil for 10 minutes, or until no longer pink and the juices run clear. Serve the remaining sauce alongside for dipping. Makes 20.

2. WASABI GRILLED SHRIMP: In a ziptop plastic bag, combine ¼ cup mirin (rice wine), 1 tablespoon fresh lime juice, and 2 teaspoons wasabi paste. Add 20 large peeled and deveined shrimp with tail intact and toss gently to coat. Seal the bag and marinate for 30 minutes. Preheat the grill or broiler. Remove the shrimp from the marinade and thread onto skewers. Discard the marinade. Grill or broil for 3 minutes, or until opaque. Remove from the skewers and place on a plate with the tails up. Makes 20.

3. CHEF GEORGE'S FILET ON A STICK: In a large zip-top plastic bag, combine 2 tablespoons olive oil, 1 tablespoon red wine or red wine vinegar, 1 clove minced garlic, 1 tablespoon cracked peppercorns, 1 tablespoon chopped fresh basil, and ¼ teaspoon salt. Add 2 beef filet mignon steaks (about ½ pound each, sliced into twenty-five 2½-inch strips) and toss to coat. Seal the bag and refrigerate for 2 to 24 hours. Preheat the broiler or grill. Soak 25 wooden skewers in cold water for 30 minutes. Remove the steak slices from the marinade and thread onto the skewers. Discard the marinade. Broil or grill 4 minutes for rare, or until desired doneness, turning once. Makes 25.

4. SALMON & CREAM CHEESE SWIRLS: In a small bowl, combine 4 ounces cream cheese with 1 teaspoon fresh lemon juice and 1 teaspoon chopped fresh dillweed. Separate and lay 4 ounces sliced smoked salmon on a work surface. If the salmon pieces are very long or thick, cut into 3- ✕ 1-inch pieces. Spread the cream cheese mixture over each piece of salmon. Roll each piece of salmon tightly to form a pinwheel and thread onto a small skewer or toothpick. Makes about 24.

5. PROSCIUTTO GRISSINI: Evenly divide ⅓ cup honey-mustard among 10 thick slices prosciutto, spreading the mustard over the slices. Cut each slice lengthwise into 3 strips. Using 30 bread sticks, wrap 1 strip prosciutto around the top ⅓ of each bread stick. Makes 30.

6. CAPONATA CROSTINI: Preheat the oven to 350°F. Cut 1 baguette into 64 slices. Place the slices on 2 baking sheets and bake for 4 minutes, or until lightly toasted. Remove from the oven and carefully rub the top of each bread slice with a clove of garlic (you will need 3 cloves total). Top each bread slice with 2 teaspoons prepared caponata and 1 teaspoon shredded Asiago cheese. Bake for 2 minutes, or until the cheese melts. Makes 64.

7. TOASTY BRUSCHETTA BITES: Preheat the oven to 350°F. In a small bowl, combine 1 cup canned black beans, rinsed and drained; 1 cup salsa, drained; and 2 tablespoons sour cream. In another small bowl, combine 3 tablespoons olive oil with 1 tablespoon chili powder. Slice 1 loaf of Italian bread into 32 slices. Place the slices on a baking sheet and brush the top side with the chili powder oil. Bake for 10 minutes, or until lightly toasted. Top each with 1 tablespoon of the bean mixture and bake until heated through, about 3 minutes. Makes 32.

8. CHEF MIKE'S LOLLIPOP CHICKEN: Preheat the oven to 425°F. In a bowl, combine 2 tablespoons olive oil, 1 tablespoon lemon juice, 1 teaspoon fresh chopped sage, 1 teaspoon fresh chopped rosemary, 1 teaspoon garlic powder, ¼ teaspoon salt, and ⅛ teaspoon pepper. Brush 6 boneless, skinless drumsticks with the mixture evenly. Wrap 1 thick slice bacon around each drumstick. Place the drumsticks on a rack in a broiler pan. Bake for 20 minutes. Increase the heat to broil and cook for 4 minutes, turning once, or until the bacon is cooked through. Makes 6 servings

9. GORGONZOLA DROPS: Preheat the oven to 375°F. Line 2 large baking sheets with parchment paper. In a medium saucepan over medium-high heat, bring 1 cup water and ½ cup butter to a boil. Reduce the heat to medium and stir in 1 cup all-purpose flour. With a wooden spoon, stir until the batter is stiff and pulls away from the sides of the pan. Add 4 eggs, one at a time, stirring well until incorporated. After the last egg has been incorporated, stir the batter until stiff. Stir in 1 cup crumbled Gorgonzola cheese. Drop by scant tablespoon onto the parchment paper, placing 1 inch apart. Bake, 1 pan at a time, for 20 to 30 minutes, or until browned and puffed. Makes about 50.

10. CHEESE TWISTS: Preheat the oven to 350°F. On a lightly floured surface, roll 1 loaf (1 pound) pizza dough to a 15- × 12-inch rectangle. Along the long side, spread ¼ cup prepared pesto and sprinkle ¼ cup shredded Italian fontina cheese over half of the dough, leaving a 1-inch border. Fold the dough lengthwise to cover the pesto. Cut crosswise into 12 strips. Twist each strip and place on a greased baking sheet. Brush with 1 beaten egg. Bake for 20 minutes, or until golden brown. Makes 12.

BUBA'S SALSA

1 jalapeño chile, quartered, seeded, and minced

½ red onion, finely chopped

1 clove garlic, minced

1½ cups fresh cilantro leaves, chopped

½ teaspoon salt

2 tablespoons lemon juice

2 cans (14.5 ounces each) petite diced tomatoes, drained

In a serving bowl, combine the chile, onion, garlic, cilantro, salt, lemon juice, and tomatoes. Toss to blend well. ***Makes 3 cups.***

COOKING TIP

Chopping is cutting food into irregular pieces about ¼ to 1 inch. To chop just a few vegetables, use a cutting board and knife. For a much larger amount, you may want to use a food processor to save time. To chop, slice the food into long strips. Lay the strips next to each other on the cutting board and slice crosswise into irregular shapes.

Dicing is cutting foods into pieces exactly the same size. Since it is not essential to delicious food and is more time consuming, dicing is not often called for in this book.

Mincing is chopping food into small (about ⅛ inch) pieces.

HOT-SELLING CALIFORNIA ROLLS

2 cups uncooked Japanese short or medium grain rice (sticky rice)

¼ cup unseasoned rice vinegar

1 tablespoon sugar

1 teaspoon salt

1 Haas avocado

1 to 2 tablespoons lemon juice

6 sheets (8- × 7-inches each) sushi nori (thin sheets of seaweed)

1 medium cucumber, peeled, halved, seeded, and cut lengthwise into six 8-inch strips

½ pound surimi (imitation frozen crabmeat), thawed if frozen and drained, cut into 12 strips

Soy sauce

Wasabi paste

Pickled ginger

Preheat the oven to 350°F.

Place the rice in a sieve and rinse under cold running water until the water runs clear.

In a medium saucepan, bring 2½ cups water to a boil. Add the rice and return to a boil. Reduce the heat to low, cover, and simmer for 15 minutes, or until all of the liquid has been absorbed. Remove the pan from the heat and let stand, covered, for 10 minutes.

Meanwhile, in a small saucepan over medium heat, combine the vinegar, sugar, and salt. Cook for 5 minutes or just until the sugar dissolves. Set aside to cool.

Evenly spread the rice into a baking pan and cover with plastic wrap to keep warm. When the rice and vinegar mixture have cooled, sprinkle the rice with the vinegar mixture using just enough to moisten the rice. Cover the rice with a damp kitchen towel to keep moist.

Halve, pit, and peel the avocado. Cut the avocado into ¼-inch slices and brush each with the lemon juice.

Place the nori sheets on a baking pan and cook for 10 minutes to soften. Keep warm.

Working with 1 sheet of nori at a time, with the long side of the sheet facing you, evenly spread with about ⅔ cup of the rice, leaving a ½-inch border on the long sides. Place ⅙ of the avocado, cucumber, and surimi horizontally down the middle of the rice. Brush the rear edge of the nori with some water. Beginning with the long side closest to you, tightly roll the nori jelly-roll style, pressing to seal the dampened end. Repeat with the remaining nori sheets, rice, avocado, cucumber, and surimi.

Using a very sharp knife, cut the rolls into 1-inch pieces. Serve with soy sauce, wasabi paste, and pickled ginger. ***Makes 48 pieces.***

SHOPPING TIP

Select cucumbers that are firm, with no blemishes or soft spots. Stick with smaller ones, which are less bitter than larger cucumbers.

THREE-CHEESE MINI CALZONES

½ pound sweet Italian sausage

1 cup fresh baby spinach leaves, washed, chopped, and drained well

½ cup part-skim ricotta cheese

¼ cup shredded mozzarella cheese

4 tablespoons shredded Parmesan cheese, divided

1 large egg yolk, beaten

1 pound refrigerated pizza dough

1 cup prepared marinara sauce, warmed

Remove the sausage from its casing.

In a large skillet over medium-high heat, cook the sausage, stirring to break up large pieces, until cooked through. Drain off any fat. Add the spinach and cook, stirring constantly, for 2 minutes, or until wilted. Remove from the heat.

Meanwhile, in a medium bowl, combine the ricotta, mozzarella, and 2 tablespoons of the Parmesan cheese. Stir in the cooled sausage mixture.

Preheat the oven to 425°F.

In a small bowl, beat the egg yolk with 1 tablespoon water. On a lightly floured surface, roll the pizza dough to a 15- × 12-inch rectangle. Using a 3-inch cookie cutter or a glass, cut out 24 circles, rerolling the dough as needed.

Place 1 tablespoon of the cheese mixture onto the center of each circle. Brush the outer edge of each with some of the egg yolk mixture. Fold each in half, forming a crescent-shaped calzone. Press the edges with a fork to seal. Place the calzones on a baking sheet. Brush the tops with the remaining egg yolk mixture and sprinkle with the remaining 2 tablespoons Parmesan cheese.

Bake for 8 to 10 minutes, or until the calzones puff and are lightly browned. Serve with the marinara sauce. ***Makes 8 servings.***

SHOPPING TIP

Mozzarella is an Italian invention, born in the countryside around Naples, where it was traditionally made from the milk of water buffalo. Today, most mozzarella is made from cow's milk.

SWEET CORN CAKES WITH PLUM TOMATO COULIS

Tomato Coulis

4 plum tomatoes, seeded and chopped

1 clove garlic, minced

½ small jalapeño chile, seeded and minced

2 tablespoons virgin olive oil

1 teaspoon sugar

Corn Cakes

1¼ cups all-purpose flour

½ cup cornmeal

1 tablespoon sugar

1 teaspoon baking powder

½ teaspoon baking soda

½ teaspoon salt

1½ cups buttermilk

¼ cup melted butter, cooled slightly

1 large egg

1 cup fresh corn kernels

To make the tomato coulis: In a medium bowl, toss together the tomatoes, garlic, jalapeño, oil, and sugar. Set aside.

To make the corn cakes: In a large bowl, whisk together the flour, cornmeal, sugar, baking powder, baking soda, and salt.

These delicious cakes are studded with fresh corn and topped with a zesty tomato mixture.

In a medium bowl, whisk together the buttermilk, butter, and egg. Add to the dry ingredients and mix just until lumpy. Fold in the corn kernels, stirring just until blended.

Heat a nonstick griddle or skillet over medium heat. Pour in the batter by 2 tablespoonfuls for each pancake onto the skillet. Cook for 1 to 2 minutes, or until the underside is golden and bubbles break on top. Turn and cook for 1 to 2 minutes more, or until the underside is golden.

To serve, place 3 pancakes on each plate and drizzle with 2 tablespoons of the tomato coulis. ***Makes 8 servings.***

COOKING TIP

For fresh corn kernels, hold a cob upright over a bowl. Slice down at a 45-degree angle to release the kernels.

Maureen Smith, formerly of Danbury, Connecticut, not only loves to cook, but eat as well!

Her Red Grape Salad recipe is one that has become her summertime signature dish, cool and easy. When Maureen is invited to a barbecue, she does not have to ask what to bring; it's already been assumed. One person, who tasted the salad for the first time, described the dish as "an explosion of flavors and textures in the mouth."

Since the cook-off, Maureen has moved to Northern California and says, "While there are many terrific supermarkets here, there's only one Stew Leonard's!"

MAUREEN SMITH'S
RED GRAPE SALAD

1 cup crème fraîche or ½ cup heavy cream and ½ cup sour cream

8 cups red seedless grapes

1½ cups crumbled Gorgonzola or blue cheese

5 ribs celery, sliced

1 cup slivered almonds, toasted (see page 32)

If making the crème fraîche, start 1 to 2 days before serving. In a medium bowl, whisk together the cream and sour cream. Cover loosely with plastic wrap and let stand at room temperature overnight, until thickened. Cover and refrigerate for at least 4 hours.

To make the salad, in a large bowl, toss together the grapes, cheese, and celery. Add the crème fraîche, tossing to coat well. Place in a serving bowl or platter and sprinkle with the almonds. **Makes 8 to 10 servings.**

BLUE RIBBON BLUE CHEESE COINS

½ cup cold unsalted butter, cut into small pieces

½ cup Saga blue cheese (about 5 ounces), cut into small pieces

⅛ teaspoon cracked black pepper

1 cup all-purpose flour

½ cup pecan halves, toasted and finely chopped

In a food processor, blend the butter and cheese until almost smooth. Add the pepper and flour and pulse just until combined. Divide the dough between 2 sheets of waxed paper and roll each into a 12-inch log. Wrap to seal and place in the refrigerator for about 1 hour, or until firm.

Preheat the oven to 350°F. Grease a baking sheet. Remove 1 log from the freezer and remove from the paper. Arrange half of the pecans on a piece of waxed paper and roll the log, pressing slightly, into the nuts. Cut the log into 16 slices. Bake the slices, cut sides down, for 15 minutes, or until lightly browned. Place the coins on a rack to cool. Repeat with the remaining log and pecans. *Makes 32 coins.*

COOKING TIP

Toasting nuts, seeds, or coconut brings out a natural sweetness and a golden-brown color. To toast in the oven, place the nuts on a baking sheet in a single layer. Toast at 350°F for 5 to 10 minutes, turning occasionally. Watch the nuts closely. To toast in a skillet, place the nuts in a single layer in the skillet and cook over medium-high heat, shaking the pan often until browned.

These salty bites are delicious with a dry red wine such as Pinot Noir or Syrah.

CRUDITÉS WITH MEDITERRANEAN DIP

1 medium orange

4 ounces cream cheese

4 ounces goat cheese

½ cup sour cream

½ small red onion, grated (about 3 tablespoons)

¼ cup grated Parmesan cheese

1 tablespoon chopped fresh rosemary leaves or 1 teaspoon dried, crushed

8 cups assorted crudités, such as carrot, bell pepper, fennel, cucumber, blanched asparagus, and green or waxed beans

Grate 1 teaspoon peel and squeeze 2 tablespoons juice from the orange. Place both in a large bowl. Add the cream cheese, goat cheese, sour cream, and onion. Using an electric mixer on low speed, beat until smooth. Fold in the Parmesan and rosemary and place in a serving bowl. Cover and refrigerate for 4 hours or overnight.

Serve the dip with the crudités. **Makes 8 to 12 servings.**

SHOPPING TIP

Goat cheese is a soft, creamy cheese with a slightly pungent flavor. Domestic goat cheeses are milder tasting than imported. To test for freshness, squeeze the cheese slightly. If it's very soft, it's fresh and mild. If it feels firm and bounces back a bit, it's a bit older and tarter. Both are delicious.

CALIFORNIA GUACAMOLE DIP

2 large ripe Haas avocados, peeled, halved, and pitted

Juice of 1 lime

¼ cup finely minced onion

2 tablespoons minced fresh or canned serrano or jalapeño chiles

¾ cup peeled, seeded, and coarsely chopped tomato

¼ cup chopped fresh cilantro leaves

½ teaspoon salt

⅛ teaspoon freshly ground black pepper

In a medium bowl, place the avocados and lime juice. Slice the avocados into chunks. With a fork, coarsely mash the avocados. Add the onion, chiles, tomato, cilantro, salt, and pepper, mixing until well blended. ***Makes 6 servings.***

SHOPPING TIP

When buying avocados, hold them in the palm of your hand and select those that seem heavy for their size. Avocados are often sold unripe, so store them on the kitchen counter until they're ripe. The fastest way to ripen avocados is in a paper bag. To determine ripeness, pull the stem off the end. If it removes easily and the flesh is green, the avocado is ripe. A brown color means it's overripe.

FRESH FRIED MOZZARELLA WITH PESTO

½ cup all-purpose flour

1 large egg beaten with 1 tablespoon water

¾ cup Italian bread crumbs

8 ounces fresh mozzarella cheese, sliced into 6 pieces

½ cup canola oil

1 tablespoon prepared pesto

½ cup sour cream

30 MINUTES OR LESS

Place the flour, egg, and bread crumbs in three separate shallow bowls. Dip the cheese into the flour. Dip into egg and coat with breadcrumbs.

Heat the oil in a large skillet over medium-high heat. When the oil is very hot, add the coated cheese and cook for 5 minutes, turning once, until golden brown. Remove with a slotted spatula to paper towels.

Combine the pesto and sour cream. Serve with the fried cheese. ***Makes 6 servings.***

SHOPPING TIP

Pesto is an uncooked sauce classically made from fresh basil, garlic, pine nuts, olive oil, and Parmesan or Romano cheese. Today, pestos are made from just about any herb, nut, oil, and cheese mixture.

For quick meals, use prepared pesto available in refrigerated sections of stores.

POPULAR POTATO CRISPS

3 tablespoons olive oil

1 pound russet potatoes (about 3 large), scrubbed

1 teaspoon dried herb such as rosemary, basil, thyme, or tarragon

1 teaspoon lemon zest

½ teaspoon salt (kosher or sea salt works best)

½ teaspoon cracked black pepper

Preheat the oven to 375°F. Brush 2 large baking sheets with some of the oil.

Using a mandoline or sharp knife, slice the potatoes crosswise into ⅛-inch slices. Arrange the potato slices in a single layer on the prepared baking sheets and brush with the remaining oil. Sprinkle with the herb, lemon zest, salt, and pepper.

Bake the slices, turning once, for 10 minutes, or until golden brown. Using a metal spatula, remove the slices from the baking sheet to a wire rack to cool completely. ***Makes 4 to 6 servings.***

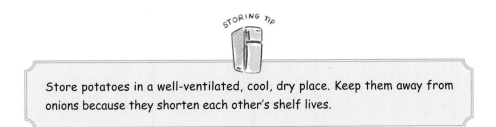

Store potatoes in a well-ventilated, cool, dry place. Keep them away from onions because they shorten each other's shelf lives.

CARAMELIZED ONION QUESADILLAS

2 tablespoons butter

1 large sweet onion, chopped

½ teaspoon dried thyme, crushed

1 tablespoon light brown sugar

1 teaspoon balsamic vinegar

2 tablespoons drained, chopped sun-dried tomatoes

4 flour tortillas (8-inch), plain, tomato, spinach, or whole wheat

1 tablespoon olive oil

1 cup shredded smoked Cheddar cheese

30 MINUTES OR LESS

Melt the butter in a large skillet over medium heat. Add the onion and thyme and cook, stirring occasionally, for 10 minutes, or until lightly browned and almost tender. Stir in the brown sugar and vinegar and cook for 10 minutes, or until very tender. Remove from the heat and stir in the tomatoes.

COOKING TIP

For a low-fat version of these quesadillas, substitute reduced-fat cheese, such as Cheddar or Monterey Jack. Omit the oil and spray the tortillas liberally with cooking spray. To pump up the fiber, use whole wheat tortillas.

Open a crisp bottle of dry Rosé wine to serve with these savory bites.

Preheat the oven to 375°F.

Brush the tops of two tortillas with half of the oil and place, oil sides down, on a large baking sheet. Evenly divide the onion mixture between the tortillas, spreading to cover. Sprinkle half of the cheese over each tortilla. Top each with another tortilla, gently pressing to seal. Brush the top tortillas with the remaining oil.

Bake, turning once, for 8 minutes, or until the quesadillas are lightly browned. Cut each into 8 wedges and serve immediately. *Makes 4 servings.*

HORSERADISH-BEEF PINWHEELS

2 tablespoons sour cream

2 tablespoons mayonnaise

2 teaspoons prepared horseradish

2 large (12-inch) flavored wraps or tortillas,
spinach or tomato

6 ounces thick deli-sliced roast beef

1 cup arugula, watercress, or spinach

1 roasted red pepper, drained and cut into strips

In a small bowl, combine the sour cream, mayonnaise, and horseradish, stirring to mix well. Set aside.

Lay 1 tortilla on a flat surface and spread with half of the horseradish mixture. Top with half of the roast beef, spread out to a thin layer. Top with half of the greens. Place half of the pepper on 1 edge of the tortilla and tightly roll the tortilla to form a cylinder. Wrap in plastic wrap and repeat with the remaining ingredients to make 2 rolls. Refrigerate for at least 4 hours or overnight.

Cut each roll into 16 slices. ***Makes 32 pinwheels (8 servings).***

EASY ITALIAN CHICKEN WINGS

24 chicken wings (about 3 pounds)
½ teaspoon salt
3 tablespoons balsamic vinegar
1 tablespoon honey
1 tablespoon Italian seasoning
1 large clove garlic, minced

Preheat the oven to 400°F. Remove and discard the tips of the chicken wings. Cut each wing through the center joint. Place the wings in a large, shallow baking pan and sprinkle with the salt. Bake the wings for 15 minutes.

Meanwhile, in a small bowl, combine the vinegar, honey, seasoning, and garlic.

Carefully remove the wings from the oven and coat with the sauce, turning the wings as you coat them. Bake for 20 minutes more, or until cooked through. ***Makes 24 wings (6 servings).***

SHOPPING TIP

Chicken is the number one meat consumed in the United States. With a subtle flavor, chicken is perfect for absorbing great-tasting marinades, rubs, and sauces.

Choose packages that have been kept very cold. The chicken should appear very fresh, with a shiny, moist-looking skin. Be sure the plastic wrap has no punctures and there is very little juice in the package.

SWEET OR SPICY MIXED NUTS

2 tablespoons light brown sugar

1 teaspoon ground cinnamon

1 teaspoon salt

1 tablespoon butter

2 cups unsalted nuts such as natural almonds, pecans, cashews, or peanuts

In a small bowl, stir together the brown sugar, cinnamon, and salt. Line a baking sheet with foil and set aside.

Melt the butter in a heavy skillet over medium heat. Add the nuts and cook, stirring frequently, for 3 minutes or until lightly browned. Add the brown sugar mixture and cook, stirring constantly, until the sugar is caramelized and lightly browned. Pour the nuts onto the prepared baking sheet, separating them. Cool the nuts on the baking sheet until room temperature.

Store the nuts in an airtight container. ***Makes 2 cups.***

COOKING TIP

Adjust the nuts and flavors to suit your family's tastes. Instead of the cinnamon, try pumpkin pie spice, cardamom, nutmeg, ginger, or a combination of them all. Or, if you prefer a spicy flavor, go for ground red pepper.

Varying the spices in this recipe can make them sweet or spicy.

SALADS AND VEGETABLES

Fresh fruits and vegetables are a cornerstone at Stew Leonard's, and they're one of the reasons why customers come from more than 50 miles away to shop in our stores, because you can't buy fresher produce unless you picked it yourself. Upon entering the produce section, customers are greeted by bins of carefully stacked tomatoes, colorful peppers, pert asparagus, and rows of fresh sweet corn.

These bountiful displays were inspired by my visits to old-fashioned farmer's markets in Europe, where everything is fresh and colorful. I love to grill vegetables in the summer, so we've included some great tips for grilling throughout this chapter.

In this chapter, you'll find some of our best-selling salad and vegetable recipes, featuring our most popular produce items. From salads like Arugula-Endive Salad with Parmesan Crisps (page 52) and Mesclun Salad with Pears and Stilton (page 55), to the Fresh Turkey and Bacon Chopped Salad (page 58), Colossal Club Salad (page 59), and Creamy Caesar Salad (page 66), which are staple stars on our in-store salad bar.

This chapter also includes 10 Winning Ways to WOW Salad Dressings (page 50) and 10 Winning Ways to WOW Mashed Potatoes (page 94).

Tomatoes on the vine surpass all other tomato sales in our stores. Our customers love them because of the aroma and taste; they're like homegrown. I love them sliced and topped with fresh mozzarella, basil, and olive oil, or for a fancier but easy to make dish, try the Stuffed Tomatoes with Spinach and Ricotta Cheese (page 82).

I hope that your family, including the youngest members, will love these vegetable recipes. To your good health!

10 Winning Ways to WOW Salad Dressings •50

Poppy Seed Dressing
Lemon-Chive Dressing
Low-Fat Ranch Dressing
Green Goddess Dressing
Honey-Mustard Vinaigrette
Simple Herb Vinaigrette
Greek Vinaigrette
Gorgonzola Vinaigrette
Light Pesto Vinaigrette
Asian Peanut Vinaigrette

10 Winning Ways to WOW

Salad Dressings

Bottled salad dressings are a great convenience, but when you're looking for unique flavors or when only the freshest will do, whip up a batch of these flavorful dressings. Store in an airtight container for up to 2 weeks. An old wine bottle with a cork works well. Doubling or tripling the recipes will save time for future meals.

1. POPPY SEED DRESSING: In a blender or food processor, combine 1 small red onion, coarsely chopped; ½ cup sugar; 1 teaspoon dry mustard; ¼ teaspoon salt; and ½ cup white wine vinegar. Process until smooth. Gradually add 1 cup vegetable oil, blending until thick and creamy. Stir in 1 tablespoon poppy seeds and 1 teaspoon grated orange peel. Makes 1 cup.

2. LEMON-CHIVE DRESSING: In a bowl, whisk together 1 cup sour cream, ¼ cup fresh lemon juice, ¼ cup chopped fresh chives, ½ teaspoon salt, ¼ teaspoon ground black pepper, and ¼ teaspoon dried mustard. Makes 1 cup.

3. LOW-FAT RANCH DRESSING: In a bowl, whisk together ½ cup low-fat mayonnaise, ¼ cup low-fat buttermilk, 2 teaspoons fresh lemon juice, 2 teaspoons Dijon mustard, 2 tablespoons chopped parsley, 2 tablespoons grated onion, ¼ teaspoon salt, and ¼ teaspoon ground black pepper. Makes 1 cup.

4. GREEN GODDESS DRESSING: In a bowl, whisk together ½ cup buttermilk; ¼ cup mayonnaise; 1 clove garlic, minced; 1 tablespoon fresh chopped parsley; 1 tablespoon fresh chopped tarragon; 1 tablespoon fresh chopped basil; ¼ teaspoon salt; and ¼ teaspoon ground black pepper. Makes ¾ cup.

5. HONEY-MUSTARD VINAIGRETTE: In a bowl, whisk together ⅓ cup white balsamic vinegar or white wine vinegar, 2 tablespoons honey-mustard, ¼ teaspoon salt, and ¼ teaspoon ground black pepper. Whisk in ½ cup olive oil. Makes 1 cup.

6. SIMPLE HERB VINAIGRETTE: In a bowl, whisk together ⅓ cup white wine, champagne, or sherry vinegar; 2 tablespoons fresh chopped herb, such as cilantro, basil, dill, parsley, or mint; 2 small cloves garlic, minced; 1 teaspoon sugar; ½ teaspoon salt; and ¼ teaspoon ground black pepper. Whisk in ½ cup extra-virgin olive oil. Makes 1 cup.

7. GREEK VINAIGRETTE: In a blender or food processor, combine ¼ cup fresh lemon juice, 1 clove garlic, ½ teaspoon dried oregano, ¼ teaspoon salt, and ¼ teaspoon ground black pepper. Process to blend. Gradually add ¼ cup olive oil until well blended. Stir in ½ cup crumbled feta cheese. Makes 1½ cups.

8. GORGONZOLA VINAIGRETTE: In a blender or food processor, combine, ¼ cup red wine vinegar, 1 clove garlic, ¼ teaspoon salt, and ¼ teaspoon ground black pepper. Process to blend. Gradually add ¼ cup extra-virgin olive oil until well blended. Stir in ½ cup crumbled Gorgonzola cheese. Makes 1½ cups.

9. LIGHT PESTO VINAIGRETTE: In a bowl, whisk together ½ cup prepared pesto, ¼ cup white balsamic vinegar or white wine vinegar, 2 tablespoons apple juice, and 2 tablespoons extra-virgin olive oil. Makes 1 cup.

10. ASIAN PEANUT VINAIGRETTE: In a blender or food processor, combine ¼ cup unsalted peanuts, ¼ cup rice wine vinegar, 2 tablespoons water, 2 tablespoons soy sauce, 1 tablespoon toasted sesame oil, and 1 clove garlic. Process to blend. Gradually add ¼ cup vegetable oil, blending until thick and creamy. Makes ½ cup.

ARUGULA-ENDIVE SALAD WITH PARMESAN CRISPS

6 ounces Parmesan cheese, coarsely shredded (about 1½ cups)

3 cups arugula leaves

3 heads endive, leaves separated and halved crosswise

1 small red onion, cut into thin wedges

1 large carrot, peeled into curls with a vegetable peeler

½ cup Simple Herb Vinaigrette (page 51) or bottled Italian dressing

Preheat the oven to 375°F.

Line 2 baking sheets with parchment paper. Place 2 tablespoons of the cheese onto the parchment paper. Using a spoon, spread into a 4-inch circle. Repeat with the remaining cheese to make 12 circles. Bake for 6 to 7 minutes, or until lightly browned around the edges.

Carefully slide the crisps onto a rack to cool slightly. Meanwhile, in a large bowl, toss together the arugula, endive, onion, carrot, and dressing. Toss to coat well. Serve the salad with the crisps. ***Makes 6 servings.***

SHOPPING TIP

Be sure to use Parmesan cheese for this recipe. A richer cheese such as Pecorino Romano may have too much fat to form the crisps.

Impress your family and friends with these Parmesan Crisps. They are actually a breeze to make!

Fruit and cheese are the perfect flavor marriage atop crisp salad greens.

MESCLUN SALAD WITH PEARS AND STILTON

1 tablespoon olive oil

2 medium Bosc pears, peeled, cored,
and cut into 1-inch slices

8 ounces mesclun or spring mix

½ cup pecan halves, toasted (see page 32)

2 ounces Stilton cheese, crumbled (about ½ cup)

½ cup Honey-Mustard Vinaigrette (page 51)

30 MINUTES OR LESS

Heat the oil in a large skillet over medium heat. Add the pears and cook, turning occasionally, for 5 minutes, or until browned and tender.

Place the mesclun in a large serving bowl. Top with the pears, pecans, and cheese. Drizzle with the vinaigrette and toss to coat well. **Makes 4 servings.**

COOKING TIP

When toasting the nuts for this salad, toast a double or triple batch. Cool and freeze the extra toasted nuts for a last-minute dish. Toasted nuts add flavor to salads, steamed vegetables, and rice dishes.

STEW'S CHOICE CAP SALAD

1 head iceberg lettuce, cleaned and chopped

1 medium green bell pepper, diced

1 medium white onion, diced

1 medium red onion, diced

3 ribs celery, diced

1 cup mayonnaise

¼ cup white vinegar

2 tablespoons sugar

½ teaspoon salt

¼ teaspoon black pepper

8 ounces green peas, shelled fresh or thawed frozen

1 can (6 to 8 ounces) water chestnuts, drained and diced

1 pound Cheddar cheese, shredded

4 ounces bacon, cooked and cut into 1-inch pieces

STORING TIP

Celery is often neglected in the fridge until it has wilted. To revive it, trim ¼ inch off the ends and place it in a glass or bowl with 2 inches of water. Cover with a plastic bag and chill. The celery will crisp up in a few hours.

In a large serving bowl, combine the lettuce, green pepper, white onion, red onion, and celery.

In a small bowl, combine the mayonnaise, vinegar, sugar, salt, and black pepper. Pour the dressing over the lettuce. Sprinkle with the peas and water chestnuts. Top with the cheese and bacon.

Refrigerate until ready to serve. Toss just before serving. ***Makes 12 servings.***

COOKING TIP

Cheese is a very useful ingredient in quick cooking. It can make a sauce creamier, add pungent flavor to a dish, or be the main source of protein in a meal.

When shredding cheese in a food processor, lightly spray the blade with nonstick cooking spray. This will prevent the cheese from forming a sticky mess on the blade.

FRESH TURKEY AND BACON CHOPPED SALAD

2 pounds cooked turkey, chopped

1 head iceberg lettuce, cleaned and chopped

3 medium tomatoes, chopped

1 pound bacon, cooked and chopped

1 cup mayonnaise

½ teaspoon salt

¼ teaspoon black pepper

Toast points or croutons (optional)

30 MINUTES OR LESS

In a large bowl, combine the turkey, lettuce, tomatoes, bacon, mayonnaise, salt, and pepper; toss to coat well. Serve with toast points or croutons if desired. ***Makes 6 to 8 servings.***

STORING TIP

Never refrigerate tomatoes of any kind. This will destroy their flavor.

COLOSSAL CLUB SALAD

4 cups chopped romaine lettuce

2 cups mesclun or gourmet salad mix

⅓ cup poppy seed dressing, prepared (or see page 50)

¼ pound ham, chopped

¼ pound turkey, chopped

¼ pound Swiss cheese, chopped

¼ pound Cheddar cheese, shredded

¼ pound bacon bits

¼ cup black olives, sliced

In a large bowl, combine the romaine lettuce and mesclun or gourmet salad mix. Top with the dressing and toss to coat well. Place on a large serving plate. Arrange the ham, turkey, Swiss cheese, Cheddar cheese, bacon, and olives in rows over the salad. ***Makes 4 to 6 serving***

SHOPPING TIP

Salad greens, including Belgian endive, Boston lettuce, radicchio, romaine, and escarole, are delicious in salads or quick sautés.

Select heads that are brightly colored, crisp, and free of browned leaves.

CHEESY CHOPPED AVOCADO SALAD

3 medium tomatoes, seeded and chopped

2 medium ripe Haas avocados, pitted, peeled, and chopped

1 large cucumber, peeled, seeded, and chopped

½ cup Simple Herb Vinaigrette (page 51), prepared with cilantro

⅓ cup crumbled cheese such as feta, blue, or Gorgonzola

In a serving bowl, combine the tomatoes, avocados, cucumber, and dressing. Toss to coat well. Sprinkle with the cheese and serve. ***Makes 6 servings.***

COOKING TIP

To quickly seed a tomato, cut the tomato crosswise in half. With your finger, scoop the seeds out to a bowl and discard.

Avocados have a large pit in the center. To remove the pit easily, cut the avocado in half lengthwise, cutting around the pit. Hold one half in each hand and turn the sides in opposite directions to separate the halves. One of the halves will hold the pit. Holding the half with the pit in one hand, carefully strike the pit with a knife, allowing the knife to stick into the pit. Gently turn the knife and remove the pit.

WARM SWEET POTATO SALAD

3 large sweet potatoes (about 3½ pounds)
2 large red onions, chopped
2 medium yellow bell peppers, chopped
2 tablespoons olive oil
½ teaspoon salt
¼ teaspoon ground black pepper
4 cups arugula
½ cup Honey-Mustard Vinaigrette (page 51)

Preheat the oven to 400°F.

Peel the potatoes and cut into 1-inch pieces. Place in a roasting pan with the onions, bell peppers, oil, salt, and black pepper. Roast for 30 minutes, turning occasionally, until tender and browned. Remove from the oven and cool in the pan for 10 minutes.

Meanwhile, place the arugula in a large salad bowl. When the potato mixture has cooled slightly, place over the arugula. Top with the vinaigrette and toss to coat well. Serve immediately. **_Makes 6 servings._**

SHOPPING TIP

Bell peppers are also known as sweet peppers and come in a variety of colors. They have become a mainstay in our diets mostly because they impart such wonderful color and flavors to dishes. Choose bell peppers that have firm flesh without soft spots. Store them in your refrigerator's vegetable crisper.

LEMON-CHIVE SPRING POTATO SALAD

1½ pounds red potatoes, scrubbed

½ teaspoon salt

¾ pound sugar snap peas, trimmed and cut diagonally in half

2 medium yellow bell peppers, cut into thin strips

1 cup Lemon-Chive Dressing (page 50)

Cut the potatoes into quarters and place in a large saucepot. Cover with cold water and add the salt. Bring to a boil over high heat. Reduce the heat to medium and boil gently for 15 minutes, or until tender. Add the snap peas during the last 5 minutes of cooking.

Drain the potatoes and snap peas in a colander and rinse with cold water. Drain completely. Place in a large bowl with the peppers and dressing and toss to coat well. Let stand for 30 minutes before serving or cover and refrigerate for 4 to 6 hours before serving. ***Makes 6 to 8 servings.***

SHOPPING TIP

For potato salads, go for the low-starch potatoes that are sometimes called waxy potatoes. Red potatoes and Eastern or Maine potatoes are examples of low-starch ones.

Try a mix of new potatoes such as red, fingerling, and purple for a colorful salad.

This twist on the classic tomato, mozzarella, and basil salad features grape tomatoes, fresh mozzarella, and cilantro.

MOZZARELLA CAPRESE SALAD

1 tablespoon red wine vinegar

2 tablespoons fresh cilantro, separated into leaves

1 clove garlic, minced

¼ teaspoon ground cumin

⅛ teaspoon salt

2 tablespoons extra-virgin olive oil

2 pints cherry or grape tomatoes, halved

½ pound fresh mozzarella cheese, cut into ½-inch cubes

In a large bowl, whisk together the vinegar, cilantro, garlic, cumin, and salt. Whisk in the oil. Add the tomatoes and mozzarella and toss to coat well. ***Makes 6 servings.***

STORING TIP

Eat Stew Leonard's fresh mozzarella the day it is purchased or the day after for the best flavor. It's a great topping for homemade pizza.

CREAMY CAESAR SALAD

½ cup skim milk

¼ cup light sour cream

¼ cup grated Romano cheese

1 tablespoon Dijon mustard

1 tablespoon fresh lemon juice

2 anchovy fillets (optional)

1 clove garlic

¼ teaspoon salt

¼ teaspoon ground black pepper

½ cup canola or olive oil

12 cups shredded romaine lettuce leaves

2 cups prepared croutons

Place the milk, sour cream, Romano cheese, mustard, lemon juice, anchovies, garlic, salt, and pepper in a food processor or blender. Process for 2 minutes, or until well blended. While the food processor or blender is running, slowly add the oil until the mixture emulsifies.

Place the lettuce and croutons in a large serving bowl. Drizzle with just enough of the dressing to coat and toss well. Reserve any remaining dressing in the refrigerator in an airtight container for up to 2 weeks. *Makes 8 servings.*

OUR CUSTOMERS' FAVORITE TUNA SALAD

2 cans (6 ounces each) tuna packed in water, well drained

1 rib celery, finely chopped

½ medium onion, finely chopped

¼ cup dried plain bread crumbs

¼ teaspoon black pepper

1 tablespoon red wine vinegar

½ cup mayonnaise

In a serving bowl, combine the tuna, celery, onion, bread crumbs, pepper, and vinegar. Stir in the mayonnaise until well blended. ***Makes 4 to 6 servings.***

COOKING TIP

Bread crumbs are used in recipes as a crisp topping, a thickener, or a binding agent.

Packaged bread crumbs are available plain and flavored, but they can be used interchangeably if necessary.

Serve this salad with salad greens or use for a sandwich filling.

MULTIPLE MUSHROOM SALAD

2 tablespoons olive oil, divided

1 medium red bell pepper, finely chopped

1 medium carrot, finely chopped

8 ounces assorted mushrooms, such as cremini, oyster, shiitake, and white, trimmed and sliced

1 teaspoon chopped fresh thyme

½ cup Gorgonzola Vinaigrette (page 51)

1 head Boston lettuce, separated into leaves

30 MINUTES OR LESS

Heat 1 tablespoon of the oil in a large skillet over medium-high heat. Add the pepper and carrot and cook, stirring frequently, for 3 minutes. Using a slotted spoon, remove to a large bowl.

Add the remaining oil to the skillet and heat over medium-high heat until hot. Add the mushrooms and cook, stirring, for 5 minutes, or until golden and any released juices have evaporated. Stir in the thyme.

Place the mushrooms in the bowl with the pepper and carrot. Toss with the vinaigrette. Place the lettuce leaves on 4 plates. Fill with the mushroom mixture. ***Makes 4 servings.***

COOKING TIP

Be sure the mushrooms are dry when adding to the skillet. Also, it's important not to crowd them, or they will steam instead of browning.

SUMMER SPINACH AND STRAWBERRY SALAD

6 cups spinach

1½ cups strawberries, hulled and halved

⅓ cup toasted, slivered almonds

⅓ cup crumbled feta cheese

⅓ cup poppy seed dressing, prepared (or see page 50)

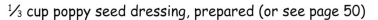

In a bowl, place the spinach. Top with the strawberries, almonds, feta, and dressing. ***Makes 4 to 6 servings.***

SHOPPING TIP

Berries are tender bites most readily available in the spring and summer months, although berries shipped from California, Florida, and South America makes it possible to eat them, especially strawberries, year round.

Select berries that are very fragrant. Be sure to turn the package upside down to look for spoilage.

SAVORY HERB-ROASTED CARROTS

1½ pounds carrots, peeled and sliced diagonally
into ½-inch pieces

1 tablespoon olive oil

½ teaspoon salt

1 tablespoon chopped fresh basil, thyme, cilantro, or dill

Preheat the oven to 400°F.

Place the carrots, oil, and salt in a large roasting or baking pan and toss to coat well. Roast, turning occasionally, for 40 minutes, or until tender and browned.

Remove the carrots from the oven and toss with the herbs. ***Makes 6 servings.***

COOKING TIP

This simple dish adds a new twist to ordinary carrots. It's a favorite among children, but adults enjoy it just as much. For a change of pace, toss with a sprinkle of Parmesan cheese.

STEW'S FAVORITE GRILLED ASPARAGUS

2 tablespoons olive oil

2 cloves garlic, minced

½ teaspoon salt

¼ teaspoon black pepper

2 pounds asparagus, trimmed

GREAT
ON THE
GRILL

Preheat the grill.

In a baking pan, combine the oil, garlic, salt, and pepper. Add the asparagus, tossing to coat well. Place the asparagus in a vegetable grill pan or directly on the grill, arranging across the grill slats. Grill for 4 minutes, turning occasionally, until tender. ***Makes 6 to 8 servings.***

STORING TIP

Store asparagus, stem ends down, in a wide glass or bowl filled with 2 inches of water. Cover with a plastic bag and refrigerate.

Asparagus spears have a tough stem bottom that should be removed before cooking. To remove, tightly hold the spear end with one hand, and with the other hand, gently snap the spear. It will break easily. Discard the tough ends.

GRILLED TUSCAN VEGETABLES

¼ cup olive oil

1 clove garlic, minced

½ teaspoon salt

¼ teaspoon black pepper

1 bulb fennel, fronds trimmed and quartered, leaving core intact

1 medium red bell pepper, quartered and seeded

4 ounces baby portabello mushrooms

1 head radicchio, quartered, leaving core intact

1 head endive, halved, leaving core intact

30 MINUTES OR LESS

GREAT ON THE GRILL

Preheat the grill.

In a small bowl, combine the oil, garlic, salt, and black pepper.

Place the fennel, bell pepper, and mushrooms in a grill rack. Brush with the oil mixture and grill for 8 to 10 minutes or until almost tender. Add the radicchio and endive and brush with the remaining oil. Grill 3 minutes longer or until the vegetables are tender and browned. **Makes 4 servings.**

SHOPPING TIP

Fennel can be sliced and added raw to salads, sautéed with other vegetables, baked, or pureed. Select firm, white fennel bulbs free of blemishes or browning and look for bright-green fronds. To slice, cut off the stems and fronds. Cut in ¼-inch slices lengthwise, cutting through the stem ends. Trim the rough ends, leaving a bit to hold them in place.

SESAME SUGAR SNAP PEAS

1 pound sugar snap peas

1 teaspoon toasted sesame oil

¼ teaspoon salt

2 teaspoons sesame seeds, toasted
(see page 32)

Bring 2 inches of water to a boil in a large saucepan over high heat. Place a steamer basket in the pan and add the peas. Cover, reduce the heat to medium, and cook for 4 minutes, or until bright green and tender-crisp. Place in a serving bowl. Toss with the oil and salt. Sprinkle with the sesame seeds. **Makes 4 servings.**

SHOPPING TIP

There are two common forms of sesame oil, which is made from crushed sesame seeds. The one called for in this recipe is dark and is known as toasted or Asian sesame oil. It has a strong flavor perfect for Asian-style dishes. The other is lighter both in color and in flavor. It is great for cooking and for salad dressings and has a subtle nutty flavor.

HOLIDAY FAVORITE GREEN BEANS ALMONDINE

30 MINUTES OR LESS

1 pound haricot vert or French green beans, trimmed

½ teaspoon salt

2 tablespoons butter

½ small onion, minced

1 clove garlic, minced

¼ teaspoon black pepper

¼ cup slivered almonds, toasted (see page 32)

In a large skillet over high heat, bring 2 inches of water to a boil. Add the beans and salt and cook for 3 minutes, or until the beans are tender. Drain the beans.

Wipe the skillet dry and place over medium-high heat. Add the butter to melt. Add the onion and cook for 3 minutes. Add the garlic and pepper and cook for 1 minute, or until lightly browned. Add the beans and almonds to the skillet, turning to coat and heat through. ***Makes 4 servings.***

STORING TIP

Store nuts at room temperature for up to a week. For longer storage, place them in the freezer in an airtight container.

STEAKHOUSE STAPLE CREAMED SPINACH

2 packages (10 ounces each) frozen chopped spinach, thawed

4 slices bacon

1 small onion, minced

2 cloves garlic, minced

2 tablespoons all-purpose flour

½ teaspoon salt

¼ teaspoon black pepper

2 cups heavy cream

Drain the spinach well and squeeze out excess moisture.

In a medium skillet, cook the bacon for 5 minutes, or until crisp. Using a slotted spoon, remove the bacon to paper towels. Add the onion and garlic to the drippings in the skillet and cook for 4 minutes, or until tender. Stir in the flour, salt, and pepper, stirring completely for 2 minutes. Gradually add the cream and stir until well blended and thickened, about 2 minutes. Add the spinach and bacon and cook until heated through. ***Makes 6 to 8 servings.***

HOW TO GET KIDS TO EAT THEIR VEGETABLES

Children love the animatronics in our produce section, like Cindy Celery and Larry Lettuce, who sing about the benefits of fruits and vegetables. Getting children to eat their veggies can be a challenge, so I've included some of my family's foolproof recipes that may quickly become favorites in your household.

For example, topping vegetables with low-fat cheese is an easy way to dress up side dishes like broccoli or cauliflower to make them more appealing to kids. My wife, Kim, puts some leftover cooked vegetables in a microwave bowl, tops them with a slice of low-fat cheese, and microwaves it for about a minute. Presto—easy, cheesy vegetables.

Here are some other quick tips.

- Serve cut-up, raw vegetables, such as peppers, carrots, and celery sticks to children with low-fat dressing for them to dip the veggies into. Many kids do not like the texture of cooked vegetables, and the addition of giving them something tasty to dip crunchy veggies into makes it fun for them to eat, too.

- Wherever possible, incorporate vegetables into the main dish recipe versus serving veggies as a stand-alone side dish. For example, incorporate roasted vegetables into macaroni and cheese (see page 109) or puree vegetables into a soup, like our Quick and Easy Creamy Carrot Soup (page 123). Try grating carrots or zucchini into muffins, such as the Low Country Corn Muffins on page 326.

- Children are more likely to eat something if they help pick it out and prepare it. Take your children grocery shopping with you and ask them to pick out a vegetable they want to eat. At home, have them help by washing the vegetables and perhaps showing them how to peel vegetables such as carrots or potatoes.

The best advice I can give to parents is not to give up. Children can be afraid to try new foods. Research suggests that the average child needs to be exposed to a new food as many as 10 times before he or she will accept it. Ask kids to just take one bite and never force them to finish something or use dessert as a bribe. Eventually, they will come around.

VERMONT CHEDDAR CAULIFLOWER GRATIN

1 large head cauliflower, cut into florets

2 tablespoons butter

1 small onion, minced

2 tablespoons all-purpose flour

2 cups 2% or whole milk

1 pound shredded cheese, such as Cheddar, Monterey Jack, or Swiss (4 cups), divided

Preheat the oven to 350°F. Grease a 3-quart baking dish.

Bring 2 inches of water to a boil in a large saucepan over high heat. Place a steamer basket in the pan and add the cauliflower. Cover and cook over medium heat for 5 minutes, or until just crisp. Remove the cauliflower and place in the prepared baking dish.

Melt the butter in a medium saucepan over medium heat. Add the onion and cook, stirring, for 4 minutes, or until tender. Stir in the flour and cook, stirring constantly, for 2 minutes. Gradually whisk in the milk and cook, stirring constantly, until thickened. Stir in 3½ cups of the cheese. Pour over the cauliflower, stirring to blend. Sprinkle with the remaining ½ cup cheese.

Bake for 25 minutes, or until bubbling and hot. ***Makes 6 to 8 servings.***

A rich cream sauce turns ordinary cauliflower into a flavorful dish.

COOKING TIP

Once you mastered the cheese sauce for this tasty kid-friendly dish, alter it to accommodate your family's tastes or what you have on hand. Broccoli and carrots may be substituted for some of the cauliflower, for example.

FRESH PROVENÇAL GRATIN

1 medium zucchini, cut into ¼-inch slices

1 medium yellow squash, cut into ¼-inch slices

2 medium tomatoes, cut into ¼-inch slices

2 small red onions, cut into ¼-inch slices

3 tablespoons olive oil

¼ cup plain bread crumbs

1 teaspoon herbes de Provence

½ teaspoon salt

½ teaspoon ground black pepper

Preheat the oven to 400°F.

Arrange the zucchini, squash, tomatoes, and onions in a large baking dish, alternating the vegetables and slightly overlapping them.

In a small bowl, combine the oil, bread crumbs, herbes de Provence, salt, and pepper. Place the mixture over the vegetables.

Roast for 30 minutes, or until tender. ***Makes 4 to 6 servings.***

SHOPPING TIP

Herbes de Provence is an aromatic blend of thyme, savory, rosemary, marjoram, oregano, and often lavender reminiscent of dishes from the south of France. Herbes de Provence is sold in various forms. Look for small stoneware crocks, tin cans, or jars in the spice sections of the supermarket.

BUTTERY BROCCOLI WITH TOASTED PINE NUTS

1 head broccoli, cut into large florets

2 tablespoons butter

¼ cup pine nuts, toasted (see page 32)

30 MINUTES OR LESS

Bring 2 inches of water to a boil in a large saucepan over high heat. Place a steamer basket in the pan and add the broccoli. Cover and cook over medium heat for 7 minutes, or until bright green and tender-crisp. Place in a serving dish.

Wipe the saucepan dry. Add the butter to the saucepan and cook for 5 minutes, or until browned. Pour over the broccoli. Top with the pine nuts. ***Makes 4 to 6 servings.***

STORING TIP

Store broccoli in a perforated plastic bag in your refrigerator's vegetable crisper for up to 5 days.

If your broccoli has gotten limp, cut ½ inch off the bottom of each stalk. Place it in a glass of cold water in the refrigerator. In a few hours it will be crisp again.

Don't discard the stems; they are loaded with flavor, nutrients, and fiber. Cut them up and add to salads, stir-fries, and sautés.

STUFFED TOMATOES WITH SPINACH AND RICOTTA CHEESE

4 large tomatoes

Pinch plus ½ teaspoon salt

3 tablespoons virgin olive oil

1 medium onion, finely chopped

1 package (10 ounces) frozen spinach, thawed, drained, and squeezed dry

¼ teaspoon freshly ground black pepper

½ teaspoon ground nutmeg

1 cup ricotta cheese

2 large egg yolks

½ cup toasted pine nuts

½ cup chopped Italian parsley

¼ cup plus 1 tablespoon grated Parmesan cheese

Preheat the oven to 350°F.

Wash and dry the tomatoes and cut off their tops. Using a melon baller or spoon, scrape out the tomato seeds and partitions, being careful not to pierce the sides of the tomatoes. Sprinkle the pinch of salt on the inside of the tomatoes and set the tomatoes upside down on a paper towel to drain.

In a skillet, heat the oil over medium-high heat. Add the onion, spinach, ½ teaspoon salt, pepper, and nutmeg. Cover and cook over low heat for about 10 minutes, stirring occasionally.

Meanwhile, in a bowl, combine the ricotta cheese and egg yolks, stirring until well blended. Add the spinach mixture, pine nuts, parsley, and ¼ cup of the Parmesan cheese.

Gently blot the insides of the tomatoes dry with a paper towel and place on a baking pan. Evenly divide the spinach mixture into the tomatoes. Top with the remaining 1 tablespoon Parmesan cheese.

Bake for 25 minutes, or until the spinach mixture is firm and heated through. Serve immediately. ***Makes 4 servings.***

SHOPPING TIP

Select tomatoes with smooth, firm skin that give a bit to pressure. Those on stems will have more flavor.

CUSTOMER RECIPE
COOK-OFF

Helen is a sewing enthusiast who enjoys making custom drapery and decorative pillows. She has been shopping at Stew Leonard's in Danbury since it first opened as an outside market. "I find that Stew's sells the freshest produce around," Helen said. "I chose to enter my Fiesta Bowl recipe because I found it to be a family favorite and a great way to get children to eat their vegetables."

HELEN KELLNHAUSER'S
FIESTA BOWL

3 plum tomatoes, chopped

1 medium onion, chopped

1 medium red or green bell pepper, chopped

1 small zucchini, chopped

1 small yellow squash, chopped

1 cob corn, kernels removed and cob discarded

1 cup cooked rice

1 package (2.5 ounces) taco seasoning

2 cups shredded Monterey Jack cheese with jalapeños, divided

5 flour tortillas (10-inch)

Prepared salsa (optional)

Prepared guacamole (optional)

Sour cream (optional)

In a large bowl, combine the tomatoes, onion, pepper, zucchini, squash, corn, and rice. Sprinkle with the taco seasoning and 1 cup of the cheese. Toss to coat well. Let sit for 15 minutes for the flavors to blend.

Preheat the oven to 375°F. Place 1 tortilla into each of 5 oven-safe small baking dishes or ramekins (about 5 inches). The tortillas should form bowls. Evenly divide the vegetables mixture among the tortillas. Top with the remaining cheese and bake for 20 minutes, or until heated through.

Serve with the salsa, guacamole, and sour cream, if desired. ***Makes 5 servings.***

ITALIAN EGGPLANT ROLLATINI

2 large eggplants, peeled and sliced lengthwise into slices (between ½ and ¼ inch each)

1 large egg

2 tablespoons chopped fresh parsley

2 tablespoons chopped fresh basil

½ teaspoon black pepper

2 cups ricotta cheese

½ cup Parmesan cheese

½ cup shredded mozzarella cheese

1½ cups marinara sauce

8 ounces fresh mozzarella cheese, cut into ½-inch slices

SHOPPING TIP

Eggplant ranges in color and size from round and white to long, narrow, and striated to the traditional purple and pear shaped.

Select eggplants that feel heavy for their size with smooth, blemish-free skin.

Preheat the oven to 375°F. Coat two baking sheets with cooking spray.

Place the eggplant slices on the baking sheets and spray the slices with more cooking spray. Bake for 10 minutes, turning once, or until the slices are lightly browned and tender.

In a small bowl, combine the egg, parsley, basil, and pepper. Add the ricotta cheese, Parmesan cheese, and shredded mozzarella cheese and stir well.

Place the eggplant slices on a single layer on a flat surface and evenly divide the filling on one end of each slice. Roll each one up like a jelly roll.

Pour the marinara sauce into a 13- × 9-inch baking dish. Place the eggplants on top of the marinara sauce and place a slice of mozzarella cheese on top of each.

Bake for 25 to 30 minutes, or until hot and bubbly. *Makes 4 to 6 servings.*

STORING TIP

Before you serve mozzarella cheese, with the wrapper on, put it in warm water for 10 to 15 minutes.

After the package is opened, you can keep mozzarella cheese in water to keep it moist in the refrigerator.

With summer squash available most of the year, this quick dish is sure to become a family favorite.

SAUTÉED SQUASH WITH OLIVE OIL AND TARRAGON

2 tablespoons olive oil

1 small red onion, halved lengthwise and sliced

1 medium zucchini, halved lengthwise
and cut into ½-inch slices

1 medium yellow squash, halved lengthwise and cut
into ½-inch slices

1 tablespoon chopped fresh tarragon

½ teaspoon salt

30 MINUTES OR LESS

Heat the oil in a large skillet over medium-high heat. Add the onion and cook for 3 minutes. Add the zucchini and squash and cook for 5 minutes, or until browned and tender. Stir in the tarragon and salt. ***Makes 4 to 6 servings.***

COOKING TIP

Tarragon is a favorite herb in French cooking, especially in fish, chicken, and vegetable dishes. It is best known for its strong anise-like flavor and should be used in moderation so that it doesn't overpower other flavors of the dish.

SAGE-ROASTED BUTTERNUT SQUASH

2 tablespoons olive oil

1 clove garlic, minced

1 tablespoon fresh or ½ teaspoon dried sage, finely chopped

1 tablespoon fresh parsley, finely chopped

¼ teaspoon black pepper

¼ teaspoon salt

2 pounds peeled and seeded butternut squash, diced

Preheat the oven to 400°F.

In a shallow roasting pan, combine the olive oil, garlic, sage, parsley, pepper, salt, and squash. Toss to coat well.

Bake for 30 to 40 minutes, or until tender and browned, turning occasionally. ***Makes 4 servings.***

SHOPPING TIP

Winter squash has a hard, inedible skin or shell. Winter squash includes acorn, butternut, Hubbard, and spaghetti.

Choose squash with smooth, firm skin that is free of soft spots.

HONEY-BAKED ACORN SQUASH

2 tablespoons butter, melted

3 tablespoons honey

2 tablespoons orange juice

1 teaspoon orange zest

2 medium acorn squash

Preheat the oven to 450°F.

In a small bowl, stir together the butter, honey, orange juice, and orange zest.

Halve the squash lengthwise and remove and discard the seeds. Cut each half lengthwise into three wedges. Place the wedges, skin sides down, in a large baking dish. Spoon the butter mixture over the squash. Cover the pan with foil and bake for 1 hour. Remove the foil and bake for 10 minutes more, or until the squash are tender. ***Makes 4 to 6 servings.***

COOKING TIP

An easy way to remove the seeds from acorn and all winter squashes is to use a melon baller.

SPAGHETTI SQUASH IN GARLIC-HERB BUTTER

1 large spaghetti squash

2 tablespoons olive oil

1 clove garlic, minced

2 tablespoons butter

2 tablespoons fresh basil

2 tablespoons fresh parsley

¼ cup grated Parmesan cheese

Salt

Black pepper

COOKING TIP

Spaghetti squash makes a great alternative to pasta. Tossed with any sauce, it makes for a hearty, satisfying meal. To prepare, cut the squash lengthwise in half. Place the squash cut sides down in a large roasting pan. Bake at 350°F for 40 minutes, or until tender. Time will vary depending on the size of the squash. Let stand until cool enough to handle. With a fork, discard the seeds and scrape the strands crosswise from the shell.

Preheat the oven to 350°F.

Split the squash lengthwise in half. Place the squash on an oiled baking sheet cut sides down and bake for 40 minutes, or until the squash pierces easily with a fork.

Remove the squash from the oven and place on a cutting board cut sides up. When cool enough to handle, discard the seeds and scrape out the flesh with a fork. Place the flesh in a serving bowl.

Heat the oil in a small skillet over medium-high heat. Add the garlic and cook for 1 minute, or until lightly browned. Remove the skillet from the heat and add the butter, basil, and parsley. Pour the butter mixture over the squash, add the cheese, toss lightly, and season with salt and pepper to taste. ***Makes 4 to 6 servings.***

SHOPPING TIP

Garlic, with its pungent flavor, is the base for many dishes.

To save time, look for peeled garlic in the refrigerator section of supermarkets. Store peeled garlic in an airtight container in the refrigerator for 2 weeks.

Garlic is easiest to mince when placed on a pinch of salt. The salt will keep the garlic from sliding off the cutting board as it's being minced.

10 Winning Ways to WOW

Mashed Potatoes

Who doesn't love mashed potatoes? They are a favorite comfort food, and for good reason. Their rich, creamy texture and hearty flavor can cure what ails you. Here you'll find two versions—our famous Rich and Delicious ones and a lighter version for all calorie counters. Either way, the added flavors will turn terrific into WOW.

1. STEW LEONARD'S RICH AND DELICIOUS MASHED POTATOES: Peel 2 pounds Idaho or russet potatoes and cut into 2-inch pieces. Place in a large saucepan with 1 teaspoon salt and cover with water. Bring to a boil over high heat. Reduce the heat to low, cover, and simmer for 20 minutes, or until tender. Drain. Place the potatoes in a large bowl with ½ cup whole milk and 2 tablespoons butter. Using an electric mixer, whip the potatoes until creamy.

2. CREAMY, LITE MASHED POTATOES: Peel 2 pounds Idaho or russet potatoes and cut into 2-inch pieces. Place in a large saucepan with 1 teaspoon salt and cover with water. Bring to a boil over high heat. Reduce the heat to low, cover, and simmer for 20 minutes, or until tender. Drain, reserving ½ cup of the potato water. Mash the potatoes with an electric mixer, ricer, or potato masher with 1 cup buttermilk and 1 tablespoon butter until creamy. Add some of the cooking water if needed.

3. WASABI MASHED POTATOES: Prepare either the Rich and Delicious or Creamy, Lite Mashed Potatoes. Stir in 2 teaspoons wasabi paste.

4. PESTO MASHED POTATOES: Prepare either the Rich and Delicious or Creamy, Lite Mashed Potatoes, omitting the butter and stirring ¼ cup pesto into the mashed potatoes.

5. TAPENADE MASHED POTATOES: Prepare either the Rich and Delicious or Creamy, Lite Mashed Potatoes, omitting the butter and stirring 2 tablespoons prepared tapenade into the mashed potatoes.

6. GARLIC MASHED POTATOES: Preheat the oven to 375°F. Cut the top quarter off of 1 bulb garlic. Brush the garlic with 1 tablespoon olive oil. Place in foil and seal tightly. Bake for 1 hour, or until browned and very tender. Meanwhile, prepare either the Rich and Delicious or Creamy, Lite Mashed Potatoes. Remove the garlic from the oven and carefully open the foil. Let the garlic sit until cool enough to handle. Squeeze each clove into the mashed potatoes and stir until well blended.

7. SAUTÉED MUSHROOM MASHED POTATOES: Prepare either the Rich and Delicious or Creamy, Lite Mashed Potatoes. While the potatoes are cooking, melt 2 tablespoons butter in a medium skillet. Add 2 minced shallots and 2 cups sliced mixed mushrooms. Sauté for 8 minutes, or until the mushrooms have released their juices and are browned and tender. Stir in 1 tablespoon chopped tarragon. Fold into the mashed potatoes.

8. CARAMELIZED ONION MASHED POTATOES: Prepare either the Rich and Delicious or Creamy, Lite Mashed Potatoes. While the potatoes are cooking, melt 2 tablespoons butter in a medium skillet. Add 1 sliced red onion and cook, stirring occasionally, for 8 minutes, or until almost tender. Add 1 bunch sliced scallions and ½ teaspoon salt and cook for 4 minutes, or until very tender and browned. Stir in 1 tablespoon balsamic vinegar. Fold into the mashed potatoes.

9. VERMONT CHEDDAR MASHED POTATOES: Prepare either the Rich and Delicious or Creamy, Lite Mashed Potatoes. Stir in 4 ounces (1 cup) shredded Vermont sharp cheddar cheese, ½ teaspoon salt, and ¼ teaspoon pepper.

10. MAPLE MASHED SWEET POTATOES: Prepare either the Rich and Delicious or Creamy, Lite Mashed Potatoes, substituting sweet potatoes for the russets. Add 2 tablespoons pure maple syrup to the mashed potatoes.

CHEF GEORGE'S UNBELIEVABLE POTATO PANCAKES

2 large russet potatoes, peeled

¾ to 1 pound pumpkin, peeled and seeded (optional)

1 medium sweet onion (such as Vidalia), quartered

¼ cup chopped parsley

2 scallions including green part, chopped

2 large eggs

½ cup all-purpose flour

½ teaspoon salt

¼ teaspoon freshly ground black pepper

3 to 5 tablespoons vegetable oil

Sour cream or applesauce

SHOPPING TIP

Onions add a pungent flavor to soups, stews, stir-fries, and more.

Select onions that are firm, without any signs of mold or soft spots.

Preheat the oven to 250°F. Place paper towels on a baking sheet.

Using a food processor or the large holes of a grater, coarsely shred the potatoes, pumpkin if using, and onion. Place in a large mixing bowl. Add the parsley, scallions, eggs, flour, salt, and pepper, tossing until well blended.

Heat 3 tablespoon of the oil in a large nonstick skillet over medium-high heat. Scoop ⅓ cupfuls of potato mixture into the pan. Cook for 3 minutes. Turn the pancakes and cook for 3 minutes longer, or until golden brown.

Place the pancakes on the prepared baking sheet and keep warm in the oven. Continue making pancakes with the remaining potato mixture, adding more oil if necessary. Top the pancakes with sour cream or applesauce. ***Makes 12 pancakes.***

SHOPPING TIP

Potatoes are among the most versatile vegetables. They are the second most-consumed food in America, with each of us eating an average of 135 pounds per year.

Select potatoes that have smooth, unblemished skins and that are firm and heavy for their size.

SWEET POTATO MOUSSE

3 medium sweet potatoes, peeled and cut into
2-inch pieces

¼ cup orange juice

1 tablespoon brown sugar

1 tablespoon honey

½ teaspoon salt

Place the sweet potatoes in a large saucepan. Cover with water and bring to a boil over high heat. Reduce the heat to low, cover, and simmer for 20 minutes, or until tender.

Drain the sweet potatoes and place in a mixing bowl. Using an electric mixer, beat on low speed until smooth. Add the orange juice, brown sugar, honey, and salt and beat until well blended. ***Makes 4 to 6 servings.***

SHOPPING TIP

Sweet potatoes are not related to white potatoes, though they are often prepared in similar fashion.

Select sweet potatoes that have firm skins without blemishes. Go for small to medium ones, which have more flavor.

GARLICKY-LEMON ROASTED POTATOES

3 pounds small Yukon gold potatoes, scrubbed and halved

2 tablespoons olive oil

½ teaspoon salt

1 tablespoon minced parsley

1 clove garlic, minced

1 teaspoon lemon zest

GREAT ON THE GRILL

Preheat the oven to 400°F.

Cut the potatoes into wedges and place in a roasting pan with the oil and salt. Toss to coat well. Roast, turning occasionally, for 40 minutes, or until tender and browned.

Meanwhile, in a small bowl, combine the parsley, garlic, and lemon zest. Place the potatoes in a serving bowl and sprinkle with the garlic/lemon mixture. ***Makes 6 servings.***

COOKING TIP

These potatoes are great prepared on the grill. Place in a grill basket or wok and cook over medium heat for 30 minutes, or until tender and browned.

DOUBLE-BAKED POTATOES

4 medium russet potatoes

¼ cup milk

3 tablespoons butter, divided

½ teaspoon salt

¼ teaspoon white pepper

1 teaspoon roasted garlic paste (see opposite page)

1 tablespoon chopped parsley

½ teaspoon paprika

1 tablespoon grated Parmesan cheese

Preheat the oven to 375°F.

Bake the potatoes for 1 hour or until tender. Place the potatoes on a cutting board for 10 minutes, or until cool enough to handle. Cut the potatoes lengthwise in half. Scoop the centers from the potatoes and place in a large bowl. Place 4 of the potato shells on a baking pan.

SHOPPING TIP

For baking or mashed potatoes, select high-starch potatoes such as Idaho, russet, or russet Burbank. Medium-starch or all-purpose potatoes are good for roasting or baking. These include Yukon gold or round white potatoes.

In a small measuring cup, place the milk and 2 tablespoons of the butter. Microwave on high for 45 seconds, or until the butter melts. Add the milk mixture to the potatoes and beat with an electric mixer for 3 minutes. Add the salt, pepper, garlic paste, and parsley. Beat until blended. Fill the reserved shells with the potato mixture.

In a small bowl, melt the remaining 1 tablespoon butter in the microwave. Brush the butter onto the potato mixture and sprinkle with the paprika and cheese. Bake for 25 minutes, or until heated through. ***Makes 4 servings.***

COOKING TIP

To make 1 teaspoon roasted garlic paste, wrap 2 unpeeled garlic cloves in tin foil. Bake at 400°F for 25 to 35 minutes, or until the garlic cloves feel soft when pressed. When the garlic cloves are cool enough to handle, squeeze the garlic paste from the peels.

PASTA, SOUPS, AND VEGETARIAN DISHES

My family loves to make soups and stews in winter. Award-Winning New England Clam Chowder (page 117) is our pride and joy. When I was growing up, my family always went digging for clams in the summer on Long Island Sound, right behind our house. We brought the fresh clams back home and made the chowder recipe created by my grandma—Anna Stewart Leonard. Grandma used heavy cream and butter from our dairy, and there was never a drop of soup left over. Now we make this soup in the stores and sell hundreds of gallons each week. One summer, we entered our chowder in the Newport Chowder Fest, and it was voted one of the top three in New England.

Pasta dishes are especially kid-friendly. This chapter features a favorite of both young and the young at heart, My Kids' Favorite Mac 'n Cheese (page 108). It's a huge seller in our stores. You'll also find 10 Winning Ways to WOW Pasta Sauces (page 106), which I hope you'll turn to again and again to whip up dinner in a flash.

Health-conscious customers have been asking for more meatless main dishes, so we've included some of our favorite vegetarian recipes including Stew Leonard's Executive Chef George's Vegetarian Picadillo (page 127), a delicious Fix-It-Fast Grilled Vegetable Hoagie (page 126), and the hearty Home-Baked Brick-Oven Pizza (page 128). I hope you enjoy these tasty dishes as much as my family does.

10 Winning Ways to WOW

Pasta Sauces

Some of the quickest home-cooked meals start with cooked pasta. Below you'll find 10 different pasta sauces; each will top 1 pound of cooked pasta. When choosing which shape to use, follow these tips. Thin pastas such as angel hair are best with light, thin sauces. Thicker shapes such as fettuccine can hold a heavier sauce, while chunky sauces are best with chunky-shaped pastas such as penne or rigatoni. When draining cooked pasta, always reserve about 1 cup of the water. If a sauce seems too thick, stir in some of the reserved water.

1. PESTO CREAM SAUCE: Drain the pasta and return the pot to the heat. Add ½ cup prepared pesto and ½ cup half-and-half and heat until warm. Add the pasta; toss and add ½ cup of the reserved water if needed.

2. ARUGULA AND TOMATO SAUCE: Heat ¼ cup olive oil in a large skillet over medium heat. Add 3 cloves garlic, minced, and cook for 3 minutes. Add 1 cup grape tomatoes, halved, and 1 pound arugula leaves, trimmed and washed. Cook, stirring, for 3 minutes or

until the tomatoes and arugula are wilted. Add ¼ cup grated Parmesan or Romano cheese. Toss with hot pasta.

3. TURKEY BOLOGNESE SAUCE: Finely chop 2 carrots, 1 onion, 1 rib celery, and 1 red pepper. Heat 2 tablespoons olive oil in a large saucepan. Cook the vegetables for 5 minutes, or until browned. Add 2 cloves garlic, minced, and cook for 2 minutes. Add 1 pound ground turkey and cook, stirring, until browned. Stir in 1 jar (24 ounces) marinara sauce, ½ cup milk, and ½ teaspoon thyme. Simmer for 20 minutes. Toss with hot pasta.

4. CREAMY CAPONATA SAUCE: In a small saucepan over medium-low heat, cook 1 cup prepared caponata until hot. Stir in ½ cup sour cream and about ½ cup reserved pasta water. Toss with hot pasta.

5. BROWN BUTTER AND SAGE SAUCE: In a small skillet, melt 6 tablespoons butter. Cook until bubbling slightly. Stir in 10 sage leaves, sliced crosswise into thin strips, and cook until the sage and butter are golden brown. Toss with hot pasta and about ½ cup reserved pasta water.

6. GARLIC AND HERB SAUCE: Heat ⅓ cup olive oil in a large skillet over medium heat. Add 3 cloves garlic, minced, and cook for 3 minutes, or until golden. Add ¼ cup fresh minced herbs such as parsley and basil. Add drained pasta and toss to coat. Add about ½ cup reserved pasta water if needed.

7. CREAMY MUSHROOM SAUCE: Melt 3 tablespoons butter in a large skillet over medium-high heat. Add 1 pound assorted sliced mushrooms, and cook, stirring, for 5 minutes, or until the mushrooms release their liquid. Stir in 1 tablespoon balsamic vinegar. Add 1 cup half-and-half and cook for 5 minutes or until thickened. Add ½ cup reserved pasta water if needed. Toss with hot pasta.

8. FRESH FAST TOMATO SAUCE: Melt 2 tablespoons butter in a large skillet over medium heat until bubbling. Add 4 large cored, seeded, and chopped tomatoes and ¼ cup chopped fresh basil. Cook for 1 minute. Remove from the heat and continue stirring for 1 minute. Toss with hot pasta and sprinkle with Parmesan cheese.

9. SESAME NOODLES: In a heatproof bowl, combine ½ cup peanut butter; 2 tablespoons lite soy sauce; 1 tablespoon toasted sesame oil; 1 tablespoon rice wine vinegar; 1 teaspoon sugar; 1 clove garlic, minced; and 1 teaspoon grated fresh gingerroot. Add ½ cup reserved pasta water, a little at a time, while whisking the mixture, until smooth. Toss with hot pasta.

10. PASTA ALLA VODKA: Heat 2 tablespoons olive oil in a skillet. Add 1 onion, chopped, and cook for 5 minutes. Add 3 cups marinara sauce and ½ cup vodka. Bring to a simmer over medium-high heat. Simmer for 5 minutes. Stir in ½ cup heavy cream and 2 tablespoons chopped fresh basil. Toss with hot pasta.

MY KIDS' FAVORITE MAC 'N CHEESE

16 ounces pasta such as elbows, shells, or farfalle

¼ cup butter

¼ cup all-purpose flour

2 cups milk

½ cup heavy cream

8 ounces Velveeta cheese, cubed

4 ounces American cheese slices, broken into strips

Preheat the oven to 350°F. Grease a 3-quart baking dish.

Prepare the pasta according to the package directions. Drain completely.

Meanwhile, in a large saucepan, melt the butter. Add the flour and cook, stirring constantly, for 1 minute. Gradually add the milk and cream and cook, stirring constantly, for about 5 minutes, or until thickened. Add the Velveeta cheese and American cheese and cook, stirring, until the cheese melts. Add the pasta, tossing to coat well.

Place the pasta mixture in the prepared pan. Bake for 30 minutes, or until hot and bubbling in the center. ***Makes 8 servings.***

COOKING TIP

Although many people pour a little oil into pasta cooking water so the pasta does not stick together, many chefs say that if you boil the pasta in a very big pot, the oil is not necessary.

Add some carrots, broccoli, and cauliflower and sprinkle 2 tablespoons bread crumbs on top of the macaroni and cheese for a heartier dish.

SPRING-STYLE PASTA

12 ounces rotelle pasta

3 tablespoons butter

2 medium carrots, cut into thin strips

1 medium red onion, cut into thin wedges

1 medium yellow bell pepper, cut into thin strips

1 bunch asparagus, cut into 2-inch pieces

1 cup heavy cream or half-and-half

¼ cup fresh basil leaves, cut into chiffonade
(see opposite page)

1 tablespoon fresh lemon juice

½ teaspoon salt

4 ounces fresh mozzarella cheese, cut into 1-inch cubes

Prepare the pasta according to the package directions.

Meanwhile, melt the butter in a large skillet over medium heat. Add the carrots and onion and cook for 5 minutes. Add the pepper and asparagus and cook for 3 minutes, or until all the vegetables are tender-crisp. Add the cream or half-and-half and over medium-high heat, bring to a boil. Boil the mixture for 4 minutes, or until reduced and slightly thickened. Remove from the heat and stir in the basil, lemon juice, and salt.

Drain the pasta and place in a serving bowl. Top with the sauce and the cheese. Toss to coat well. ***Makes 4 to 6 servings.***

Omit the cream sauce and toss with marinara sauce to reduce the fat and calories in this dish.

COOKING TIP

Chiffonading is cutting vegetables (usually herbs, spinach, or lettuces), into thin strips.

Arrange a stack of clean leaves. Roll the leaves to form a "log." Cut crosswise down the log to form thin strips.

Stew Leonard's
CUSTOMER RECIPE
COOK - OFF

Amy always enjoyed watching her mother and grandmother cook when she was growing up. Although eating their meals was Amy's favorite part, she developed an interest in cooking like they did. Amy was not alone— cooking has become a popular activity in her family. Amy's brother, sister, and she enjoy trying to re-create versions of their family's favorite recipes as a way to revisit the times when they were young.

"I have been shopping at Stew Leonard's in Danbury, Connecticut, for many years," says Amy. "Although it is a far drive, the quality and selection of fresh products makes it worth the trip, particularly when it comes to making my Shrimp and Penne with Asiago Cream Sauce. This dish is also very versatile and can please just about any taste palate."

SHRIMP AND PENNE WITH ASIAGO CREAM SAUCE

12 ounces penne pasta

2 tablespoons olive oil

1 pound medium shrimp, peeled and deveined

¼ cup chicken broth

1 tablespoon minced parsley

1 cup heavy cream

1 cup Asiago cheese, divided

Prepare the pasta according to the package directions.

Heat the oil in a large skillet over medium-high heat. Add the shrimp and cook, turning occasionally, for 4 minutes, or until almost cooked. Add the broth, parsley, and cream and bring to a simmer. Simmer, uncovered, for 3 minutes. Stir in ¾ cup of the cheese.

Drain the pasta and place in a large serving bowl. Toss with the cream sauce. Sprinkle with the remaining ¼ cup cheese. **Makes 4 to 6 servings.**

TUXEDO PASTA WITH ROASTED EGGPLANT

12 ounces bow-tie pasta

1 small eggplant, peeled and cut into 1½-inch cubes

1 medium onion, chopped

1 medium green bell pepper, chopped

4 tablespoons extra-virgin olive oil, divided

2 cloves garlic, minced

1 can (28 ounces) crushed tomatoes or Italian peeled tomatoes

¼ cup pitted calamata olives, chopped

1 tablespoon chopped fresh thyme or 1 teaspoon dried, crushed

Preheat the oven to 350°F. Prepare the pasta as the package directs.

Meanwhile, place the eggplant, onion, and pepper in a large roasting pan. Toss with 3 tablespoons of the oil. Roast, turning occasionally, for 35 minutes, or until tender and browned.

In a large skillet, heat the remaining 1 tablespoon oil over medium heat. Add the garlic and cook for 2 minutes, stirring constantly. Add the tomatoes, olives, and thyme and bring to a boil. Reduce the heat to low and simmer, uncovered, for 10 minutes. Add the eggplant mixture.

Place the pasta in a large serving bowl and top with the eggplant sauce. Toss to coat well. ***Makes 4 servings.***

HEARTY PASTA E FAGIOLI

2 tablespoons extra-virgin olive oil

2 cloves garlic, minced

1 medium yellow onion, chopped

1 can (35 ounces) crushed tomatoes

1 cup vegetable or chicken broth

½ teaspoon dried basil, crushed

¼ teaspoon dried oregano, crushed

8 ounces ditalini, elbow, or small shell pasta

1 can (14 to 16 ounces) cannellini beans, rinsed and drained

Grated Parmesan cheese (optional)

In a large skillet, heat the oil over medium-high heat. Add the garlic and onion and cook, stirring, for 4 minutes, or until softened. Add the tomatoes, broth, basil, and oregano. Bring to a boil.

Stir in the pasta and beans and cook for 10 minutes, or until the pasta is tender.

Serve with Parmesan cheese, if desired. ***Makes 4 servings.***

COOKING TIP

When a soup or stew such as this calls for pasta, cook it right in the dish instead of in another pot. Simply add a bit more liquid, such as the broth here, and the pasta will cook while the flavors are blending.

CHILLED TUSCAN BREAD SOUP

2 tablespoons olive oil

1 large onion, chopped

1 clove garlic, minced

¼ cup basil leaves, cut into thin strips

½ teaspoon salt

¼ teaspoon black pepper

3 to 4 pounds fresh large plum tomatoes, cored, seeded, and chopped

32 ounces chicken broth

½ loaf Ciabatta or Italian bread, cut into 1-inch pieces

In a large saucepan, heat the oil over medium-high heat. Add the onion and cook, stirring, for 10 minutes, or until golden brown. Add the garlic, basil, salt, and pepper and cook for 2 minutes.

Add the tomatoes and broth and bring to a boil. Remove from the heat.

Allow the soup to cool. Place in a serving bowl and cover with plastic wrap. Refrigerate until cold.

To serve, ladle some soup in a bowl and top with some bread pieces.

Makes 8 servings.

SHOPPING TIP

Ciabatta bread, a bestseller of Stew Leonard's, is a long, roughly oval shaped flat bread. It is ideal for making pizzalike appetizers. Cut the ciabatta length-wise through the center and add your favorite toppings, then bake or broil.

AWARD-WINNING NEW ENGLAND CLAM CHOWDER

4 tablespoons butter

2 medium onions, diced

1/4 cup all-purpose flour

1/2 teaspoon salt

1/4 teaspoon freshly ground black pepper

16 ounces clam juice

1 cup milk

1/2 cup heavy cream

2 cups cubed potatoes, peeled (about 4 medium potatoes)

4 cans (6 1/2 ounces each) chopped clams

In a large saucepan, melt the butter over medium-high heat. Add the onions and cook for 5 minutes, or until the onions are tender. Add the flour, salt, and pepper and cook, stirring constantly, for 1 minute. Gradually add the clam juice, milk, and cream. Bring to a simmer. Add the potatoes and simmer for 10 minutes, or until the potatoes are tender. Add the clams and cook for 3 minutes, or until heated through. ***Makes 4 to 6 servings.***

CHEF GEORGE'S VELVETY LOBSTER BISQUE

1 fresh lobster (about 1½ pounds)

2 tablespoons olive oil

1 shallot, minced

1 carrot, diced

1 rib celery, diced

1 leek (white part only), chopped

1 clove garlic, minced

1 tablespoon Cognac

2 cups chopped fresh tomatoes

2 tablespoons tomato paste

½ cup rice

½ tablespoon fresh tarragon, chopped

½ tablespoon fresh thyme, chopped

½ teaspoon salt

¼ teaspoon cracked black pepper

⅛ teaspoon ground red pepper

1 bay leaf

2 cups heavy cream

Fill a large pot of water and bring to boiling. Add the lobster, head first, and cook for 10 minutes, or until the lobster is completely red. Using tongs, remove the lobster to a bowl. Set aside to cool slightly. Reserve 4 cups of the cooking water.

Meanwhile, in a large saucepan, heat the oil over medium-high heat. Add the shallot, carrot, celery, leek, and garlic. Cook, stirring, for 5 minutes. Add the Cognac and cook, stirring constantly, for 2 minutes. Add the reserved lobster water, 2 cups additional water, tomatoes, tomato paste, rice, tarragon, thyme, salt, black pepper, red pepper, and bay leaf. Bring to a boil. Reduce the heat to low, cover, and simmer for 25 minutes.

While the soup is cooking, shell and cut the lobster into bite-sized pieces.

Remove and discard the bay leaf. Place the mixture in a blender and puree. Return to the pan and add the cream. Bring to a simmer. Add the lobster and serve. ***Makes 8 servings.***

COOKING TIP

Lobsters can release much liquid while you are cracking the shells. To prevent this, once you have removed them from the hot water, hold them over the pot of water (tongs work well) and, using kitchen shears, snip the ends of the claws. The water will drip into the pot, and you won't lose any precious meat.

ZESTY CUBAN BLACK BEAN SOUP

1 pound dried black beans, rinsed and picked over

64 ounces chicken broth

2 tablespoons olive oil

2 carrots, diced

2 ribs celery, diced

1 large onion, diced

2 cloves garlic, minced

½ pound ham, diced

1 teaspoon Cajun spice mix or ground cumin

1 bunch scallions, thinly sliced

2 cups chopped cilantro

Place the beans in a large bowl and cover with cold water. Let soak overnight. Or place the beans in a large saucepan and cover them with cold water. Bring the water to a boil over high heat. Boil for 5 minutes.

SHOPPING TIP

Scallions are a member of the onion family and are also know as green onions or spring onions.

Select scallions with firm, white bulbs and crisp, bright-green tops.

Remove the beans from the heat, cover, and let sit for 1 hour. Drain the beans.

In a large saucepot, place the beans and broth over high heat. Bring to a boil. Reduce the heat to low, cover, and simmer for 2 to 2½ hours, or until the beans are tender.

In a skillet, heat the oil over medium-high heat. Add the carrots, celery, and onion and cook, stirring, for 4 minutes. Add the garlic and cook for 2 minutes, or until the vegetables are browned. Add the ham and Cajun spice mix or cumin and cook for 5 minutes. Add to the beans and simmer for 15 minutes. Remove from the heat and stir in the scallions and cilantro. ***Makes 8 servings.***

STORING TIP

Store onions in a cool, dry place with good ventilation for up to a month. Keep them away from potatoes because they shorten each other's lives. Discard any onions that have sprouted.

This rich creamy soup gets its body from pureed carrots and apple. Its zest comes from grated ginger and curry powder.

QUICK AND EASY CREAMY CARROT SOUP

2 tablespoons olive oil

1 medium yellow onion, chopped

2 teaspoons curry powder

1 pound carrots, cut into 1-inch pieces

4 cups vegetable broth

1 large apple, such as Granny Smith, Braeburn, or Gala

1 tablespoon grated gingerroot or 1 teaspoon ground ginger

1 cup prepared croutons

Heat the oil in a large saucepan over medium-high heat. Add the onion and cook, stirring, for 4 minutes. Stir in the curry powder and cook for 1 minute. Add the carrots and broth and bring to a boil.

Reduce the heat to low, cover, and simmer for 20 minutes, or until the carrots are just tender. Add the apple and gingerroot and cook for 10 to 20 minutes longer, or until the carrots and apple are very tender. Remove from the heat and let cool for about 10 minutes.

Working in batches, place the mixture in a food processor or blender. Process until smooth. To serve, top each bowl with some of the croutons. ***Makes 4 to 6 servings.***

SHOPPING TIP

For the fastest carrots, opt for bags of pre-peeled baby carrots. You can slice, grate, or chop these without having to spend time peeling.

MIDDLE-EAST TABBOULEH-STUFFED TOMATOES

1 cup bulgur wheat
½ cup fresh lemon juice
1 teaspoon salt, divided
6 large tomatoes
1 medium yellow bell pepper, finely chopped
4 scallions, sliced
½ cup chopped fresh parsley
1 tablespoon chopped fresh tarragon
¼ cup extra-virgin olive oil
¼ teaspoon ground black pepper
8 ounces fresh mozzarella cheese, cut into ¼-inch cubes

30 MINUTES OR LESS

Place the bulgur in a large bowl and pour 1½ cups boiling water over it. Stir in the lemon juice and ½ teaspoon of the salt and let stand for 30 minutes, or until almost all of the liquid is absorbed.

Meanwhile, slice off the top ¼ of the tomatoes. Cut the center pulp out of the tomatoes, leaving a ¼-inch shell. Seed the pulp and chop. Place the chopped tomato in a large bowl. Add the bell pepper, scallions, parsley, tarragon, oil, pepper, and remaining ½ teaspoon salt. Toss to blend. Add the bulgur or couscous and cheese; toss to coat well. Place the tomato shells on a serving plate. Fill the tomatoes with the tabbouleh mixture. *Makes 6 servings.*

PEARS AND PECAN HOLIDAY STUFFING

3 tablespoons butter, divided

2 ribs celery, chopped

1 large red onion, chopped

2 medium red and/or green pears, halved, cored, and cut into ½-inch pieces

1 tablespoon chopped fresh thyme or 1 teaspoon dried thyme, crushed

½ teaspoon salt

½ teaspoon ground black pepper

1 loaf Italian or whole grain bread for stuffing (about 10 ounces), torn into pieces (about 6½ cups)

2 cups toasted (see page 32) pecans, coarsely chopped

2 cups vegetable or chicken broth

Preheat the oven to 325°F. Butter a 3-quart baking dish with 1 tablespoon of the butter.

In a large skillet, melt the remaining 2 tablespoons butter over medium-high heat. Add the celery and onion and cook for 8 minutes, or until tender. Add the pears, thyme, salt, and pepper and cook, stirring constantly, for 4 minutes, or until lightly browned. Place in a large bowl. Add the bread and pecans to the bowl and toss to blend. Sprinkle with the broth, tossing to coat well. Place in the prepared baking dish. Bake for 45 to 55 minutes, or until the top is golden brown. ***Makes 8 to 10 servings.***

FIX-IT-FAST GRILLED VEGETABLE HOAGIE

2 tablespoons olive oil

2 cloves garlic, minced

2 tablespoons chopped fresh rosemary

½ teaspoon salt

1 small eggplant, cut lengthwise into ½-inch slices

1 large red onion, cut crosswise into ½-inch slices

1 medium zucchini, cut lengthwise into ½-inch slices

8 ounces fresh mozzarella cheese, cut into 8 slices

1 long loaf semolina or Italian bread, sliced in half lenghwise

1 large tomato, cut crosswise into ½-inch slices

30 MINUTES OR LESS

GREAT ON THE GRILL

Brush the grill rack or a rack set in a broiler pan with oil. Preheat the grill or broiler.

In a small bowl, combine the oil, garlic, rosemary, and salt. Place the eggplant, onion, and zucchini on a large plate. Brush the vegetables with the oil mixture and grill or broil, turning, for 10 minutes, or until tender.

Place half of the cheese on the bottom bread half and top with the grilled vegetables. Top the vegetables with the remaining cheese, tomato slices, and the bread top. Cut diagonally into slices. ***Makes 6 to 8 servings.***

CHEF GEORGE'S VEGETARIAN PICADILLO

1 cup long-grain rice

2 tablespoons olive oil

1 medium onion, chopped

2 cloves garlic, minced

1 medium zucchini, quartered lengthwise and sliced

1 medium red bell pepper, chopped

1½ cups canned whole tomatoes in thick puree

1 can (14 to 19 ounces) black beans, rinsed and drained

⅓ cup raisins

⅓ cup pimiento-stuffed green olives, sliced

½ teaspoon ground cinnamon

¼ teaspoon ground cloves

30 MINUTES OR LESS

Prepare the rice according to the package directions.

Heat the oil in a skillet over medium-high heat. Add the onion and cook for 3 minutes. Add the garlic, zucchini, and pepper and cook for 5 minutes, stirring, or until lightly browned. Add the tomatoes, beans, raisins, olives, cinnamon, and cloves. Bring to a simmer. Reduce the heat to medium-low and simmer for 10 minutes, or until heated through and blended. Serve over the rice. **Makes 4 servings.**

HOME-BAKED BRICK-OVEN PIZZA

1 medium yellow bell pepper, halved and cored

1 medium red onion, cut in quarters through the root end

3 tablespoons olive oil, divided

2 tablespoons balsamic vinegar

1 tablespoon honey-mustard

2 cups mixed salad greens

1 pound refrigerated pizza dough, thawed

8 ounces soft goat cheese, such as chèvre or Montrachet

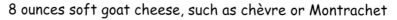

30 MINUTES OR LESS

GREAT ON THE GRILL

Preheat the grill. Coat the grill rack with oil.

Brush the pepper and onion with 1 tablespoon of the oil. Place on the grill and cook, turning occasionally, for 5 minutes, or until lightly charred. Set on a cutting board to cool slightly. Cut into thin strips.

Meanwhile, in a large bowl, whisk together the remaining 2 tablespoons oil and the vinegar and mustard. Add the salad greens and the grilled pepper and onion and toss to coat well.

Divide the dough into 6 pieces. Roll each on a lightly floured surface until ⅛ inch thick. Recoat the grill rack with oil and place 3 of the dough rounds on the grill. Cook for 2 to 3 minutes, or until the top bubbles slightly. Using tongs, turn the dough and cook for 1 to 2 minutes longer, or until lightly browned. Remove to a baking sheet. Repeat with the remaining dough.

Grilling adds a smoky flavor to pizza while creating a thin, crisp crust.

Evenly divide half the goat cheese over the crusts. Top each with the salad mixture and remaining cheese. Using a large metal spatula, slide the pizzas back on the grill. Cook for 1 minute to wilt the salad and melt the cheese. ***Makes 6 servings.***

COOKING TIP

Grilled pizzas can be enjoyed all summer long. To make a traditional Margherita Pizza, top the dough with mozzarella cheese, chopped Roma tomatoes, and basil instead.

BEEF, VEAL, AND PORK

From Stew Leonard's famous fork-tender filet mignon that is our number one selling item year round, to our aged beef cases, normally only found in high-end steakhouses, customers rely on the high-quality beef, veal, and pork sold in our stores.

We searched America's heartland and handpicked the best cattle ranchers to supply us with the more than 50 tons of fresh beef we sell each week in our stores. Stew Leonard's receives daily deliveries of beef, so we can guarantee that we not only have the largest selection, but also the best quality available. If you don't see something you're looking for in our meat cases, one of our 30 expertly trained butchers will custom cut it for you.

In this chapter, we give you 10 Winning Ways to WOW Filet Mignon (page 134) with delectable sauces that are easy to prepare, such as our wild mushroom sauce. Another favorite, sirloin steak, is fabulously featured in the Customer Cook-Off Recipe Steak Tuscany (page 147).

Ground beef is a popular choice for quick dinners. To ensure its freshness, we grind our ground chuck and sirloin hourly. In this chapter, you'll find favorite ground beef recipes, including Pepper-Cups with Beef and Rice (page 150) and Meatballs with Fresh Mozzarella (page 155).

Veal is a versatile meat, featured here in several recipes, including Lemon Parsley Veal Piccata (page 158) and Veal Scaloppine with a Touch of Vino (page 160).

Over the years, pork has gained popularity across the country. To meet this need, we present some customer favorites: Ginger-Marinated Pork Tenderloin (page 166) and Pork Chops with Granny Smith Applesauce (page 168).

Bon appétit!

10 Winning Ways to WOW

Filet Mignon

Filet mignon, beef tenderloin cut into 1- to 2-inch steaks, is a favorite at Stew Leonard's. These tender steaks should be cooked quickly. Many folks like them cooked to medium-rare or 145°F on an instant-read thermometer. Follow one of these cooking methods to prepare the simply delicious recipes below.

*To **pan-sear filets**, season 4 filets with ½ teaspoon salt and 1¼ teaspoon ground black pepper. Heat 1 tablespoon butter in a large, heavy skillet over medium-high heat and cook the steaks, turning once, for 5 minutes, or until of desired doneness.*

*To **grill filets**, lightly oil a grill rack. Cook the filets, turning once, for 6 minutes, or until of desired doneness.*

*To **broil filets**, place the filets on a rack in the broiler pan. Broil 4 inches from the heat source, turning once, for 10 minutes, or until of desired doneness.*

1. FILET MIGNON WITH COGNAC-PEPPERCORN SAUCE: Pan-sear 4 filets. Remove the filets from the skillet and keep warm. Over medium high heat, add 1 tablespoon butter; 5 shallots, minced; and 1 tablespoon dried peppercorn mixture to the skillet and cook for 1 minute. Stir in ⅓ cup cognac or brandy and cook for 1 minute, stirring to deglaze. Stir in 1 cup heavy cream. Bring to a boil. Reduce the heat to low and simmer for 5 minutes, or until thickened. Serve over the filets.

2. FILET MIGNON WITH WILD MUSHROOM SAUCE: Pan-sear 4 filets. Remove the filets from the skillet and keep warm. Over medium-high heat, add 1 tablespoon butter and ½ pound fresh assorted mushrooms to the skillet and cook for 5 minutes or until the mushrooms have released their juices. Add 3 shallots, minced, and cook for 1 minute. Add ½ cup red wine and ½ cup beef broth. Bring to a boil; reduce the heat to low and simmer for 5 minutes, or until thickened. Serve over the filets.

3. SPICE-RUBBED FILETS: In a small bowl, combine 1 clove garlic, minced; ½ teaspoon salt; ½ teaspoon chili powder; ½ teaspoon dried oregano leaves; ¼ teaspoon cumin powder; and ¼ teaspoon ground black pepper. Rub the mixture

over 4 filets. Place on a plate, cover with plastic wrap, and refrigerate 1 to 24 hours. Grill or broil.

4. ISLAND-STYLE FILETS: In a zip-top plastic bag, combine ¼ cup fresh lime juice; 1 tablespoon brown sugar; 1 tablespoon minced fresh ginger; 2 cloves garlic, minced; and ½ teaspoon salt. Add 4 filets,

seal, and turn to coat. Refrigerate for 1 to 24 hours. Grill or broil the filets and serve with prepared mango chutney.

5. BACON-WRAPPED FILETS: In a small bowl, combine ¼ teaspoon each crushed dried rosemary, salt, and ground black pepper. Season 4 filets with the herb mixture. Partially cook 4 strips bacon to cook off some of the fat, but do not crisp. Wrap the bacon around the filets and grill or broil.

6. GORGONZOLA FILETS: In a small bowl, combine 1 teaspoon cracked black pepper; 1 clove garlic, minced; and 1 teaspoon dried thyme leaves, crushed. Rub into 4 filets. Pan-sear the filets. Remove to a plate to keep warm. Add ½ cup beef broth and ⅓ cup dry red wine to the same pan. Over medium-high heat, bring to a boil and cook for 2 minutes, stirring to release the browned bits. Remove from the heat and stir in 4 ounces Gorgonzola cheese. Serve over the filets.

7. CARAMELIZED ONION FILETS: In a large skillet, heat 2 tablespoons butter over medium-high heat. Add 2 large yellow and/or red onions, halved and sliced; ¼ teaspoon salt; and ⅛ teaspoon ground black pepper. Cook over medium heat for 20 minutes, or until browned and very tender. Stir in 1 tablespoon balsamic vinegar. Remove to a bowl and keep warm. Pan-sear 4 filets in the same skillet and serve over a bed of the onions.

8. SOY-GINGER FILETS: In a shallow bowl, combine ¼ cup soy sauce, ¼ cup rice wine vinegar, 2 tablespoons toasted sesame oil, 2 tablespoon grated fresh ginger, and 1 clove garlic, minced. Add 4 filets and marinate for 20 minutes. Remove the filets, allowing the marinade to drip back into the bowl. Reserve the marinade. Grill or broil the filets. Meanwhile, place the reserved marinade in a small saucepan. Bring to a boil over high heat and boil for 5 minutes. Serve with the filets.

9. ROASTED RED PEPPER SAUCED FILETS: Pan-sear 4 filets. Remove the filets from the skillet and keep warm. Add 1 tablespoon butter to the skillet and cook 1 shallot, minced, for 2 minutes. Stir in 1 jar (3 ounces) roasted red peppers, drained and chopped; 1 tablespoon chopped fresh basil; 1 teaspoon white wine vinegar; 1 teaspoon sugar; and ½ teaspoon salt. Cook for 2 minutes to heat through. Place mixture in a blender or food processor and puree. Serve over the filets.

10. GRILLED FILET SALAD: This recipe is a great way to use the tips of a whole tenderloin. Cut the meat into 1-inch strips. Pan-sear, cooking for 1 to 2 minutes, or until browned. Remove from the skillet. Arrange mesclun or spring mix salad in a large bowl. Top with the meat and drizzle with Greek Vinaigrette (page 51) or Gorgonzola Vinaigrette (page 51).

THREE-HERB-CRUSTED FLANK STEAK

2 cloves garlic, minced

1 tablespoon chopped fresh rosemary

1 tablespoon chopped fresh thyme

½ teaspoon salt

½ teaspoon ground black pepper

1 tablespoon olive oil

1 tablespoon lemon juice

1 flank steak (about 1½ pounds)

WINE PAIRING

Cabernet or red Bordeaux

30 MINUTES OR LESS

GREAT ON THE GRILL

Preheat the grill or broiler.

In a small bowl, stir together the garlic, rosemary, thyme, salt, pepper, oil, and lemon juice. Place the steak on the grill rack or a rack in a broiler pan. Top with half of the herb mixture.

Grill or broil (4 inches from the heat source) for 5 minutes. Turn the steak and brush with the remaining herb mixture. Grill or broil for 5 minutes, or until an instant-read thermometer inserted in the center registers 145°F for medium-rare. ***Makes 8 servings.***

COOKING TIP

If time permits, you may marinate this steak overnight. Place in a zip-top plastic bag and top the steak with half of the herb mixture. Turn and top with the remaining herb mixture. Seal the bag and refrigerate for 6 to 24 hours.

HERBED BEEF TENDERLOIN WITH TAWNY PORT SAUCE

2 shallots, minced

2 tablespoons chopped fresh thyme

1 tablespoon chopped fresh rosemary

1 teaspoon freeze-dried pink peppercorns, crushed

1 tablespoon olive oil

½ teaspoon salt

½ teaspoon ground black pepper

1 trimmed beef tenderloin (4 to 5 pounds)

2 cups beef broth

½ cup tawny port

4 tablespoons butter, cut into pieces

WINE PAIRING

Cabernet or Merlot

Preheat the oven to 400°F.

In a small bowl, combine the shallots, thyme, rosemary, and peppercorns, stirring to blend well. Remove 1 teaspoon of the herb mixture and place in a small saucepan. Set aside.

Add the oil, salt, and pepper into the bowl with the herb mixture, blending to form a paste. Rub the herb mixture over the beef roast and place the roast in the center of a roasting pan.

Roast the beef for 30 minutes, or until an instant-read thermometer in-

Sweet port wine combines with fresh herbs and savory peppercorns for a rich sauce worthy of the king of beef.

serted in the center registers 135°F for rare, 145°F for medium-rare, or 160°F for medium well-done.

Meanwhile, add the broth and port to the saucepan with the herb mixture. Place over high heat and bring to a boil. Boil until reduced to about 1½ cups, about 30 minutes.

When the roast is done, remove to a cutting board and let stand for 10 minutes. Pour the pan drippings into the sauce. Bring to a boil. Remove the pan from the heat and whisk in the butter. Serve with the sliced beef. ***Makes 8 to 10 servings.***

SHOPPING TIP

Pink peppercorns aren't really peppercorns but berries. They are available either freeze-dried (as called for in this recipe) or packed in water or brine. Quite mild whole, when ground they have a sweet delicate flavor with a peppery taste and aroma.

CUSTOMER RECIPE
COOK-OFF

Lois has been a Stew Leonard's shopper for the 7 years she has lived in Connecticut. She shops at Stew's, she says, because "aside from its being a unique shopping experience, I know that the fish is fresh (very important), and the filet mignons are an excellent-quality meat that's priced right. But most of all, I get to break my diet with some sample cookies!" The fudge brownie cookies are her favorite.

Lois chose to enter this recipe because Stew Leonard's is the only place she will buy filet mignon. The dish is always a crowd-pleaser at her dinner parties, and it's easy to prepare. It's delicious served with salsa and corn chips.

Lois works as a dental assistant and volunteers for the Newtown Junior Women's Club. She is also a member of the Duffle Bag, a living-history group that honors the veterans of World War II.

LOIS BARBER'S
TEX-MEX FILET MIGNON

2 tablespoons olive oil

3 cloves garlic, crushed

1 medium onion, sliced

2 or 3 Mexican peppers of different color, variety, and/or hotness, sliced into thin strips; or 1 small can mild Mexican chile peppers

4 ounces Monterey Jack cheese, shredded (about 1 cup)

6 ounces Cheddar cheese, shredded (about 1½ cups)

8 filet mignon steaks (about 1½ inches thick)

Salt

Ground black pepper

Prepared salsa

Preheat the grill. Brush the grill rack with olive oil. Heat the oil in a medium skillet over medium-high heat. Add the garlic and cook for 2 minutes. Add the onion and peppers and cook over medium heat, stirring occasionally, for 5 minutes, or until the onions are tender. Stir in the Monterey Jack and Cheddar cheeses, cover, and remove from heat.

Place the filets flat on a work surface. Holding a knife parallel to the surface, cut a crosswise slice through the meat to 1 inch from the sides. Open the steak like a book and pound the sides with a flat mallet. Sprinkle with salt and pepper. Evenly divide the cheese and pepper mixture onto one side of each of the steaks. Fold the other side over the filling and press along the edge to seal. Grill the filets, turning once, for 6 minutes for medium-rare doneness.

Serve with the salsa spooned over the steaks. ***Makes 8 servings.***

TENDER FILET OF BEEF WITH CRABMEAT CRUST

6 beef filets, at room temperature (6 ounces each)

1½ teaspoons salt, divided

1¼ teaspoons freshly ground black pepper, divided

1 tablespoon olive oil

½ cup finely chopped yellow onion

¼ cup finely chopped green bell pepper

¼ cup finely chopped celery

2 tablespoons finely chopped parsley, divided

1 tablespoon finely chopped scallions

½ pound lump crabmeat, picked over for shells and cartilage

2 tablespoons mayonnaise

¼ cup bread crumbs

WINE PAIRING

Pinot Noir

GREAT ON THE GRILL

Preheat the grill or a grill pan to high. Preheat the oven to 450°F.

Season the filets with 1 teaspoon of the salt and 1 teaspoon of the black pepper. Mark the filets on the grill, searing fully on both sides. Transfer the filets to a small baking sheet and set aside.

In a medium skillet, heat the oil over medium-high heat. Add the onion, bell pepper, celery, the remaining ½ teaspoon salt, and the remaining ¼ teaspoon black pepper and cook, stirring occasionally, until the vegetables are tender, about 5 minutes. Add 1 tablespoon of the parsley and the scallions and cook until wilted, about 1 minute. Remove from the heat.

Place the crabmeat in a medium bowl and add the cooked vegetables. Add the mayonnaise and bread crumbs and stir gently to combine. Evenly divide the crabmeat between the filets, allowing about ¼ cup for each steak. Pack the crabmeat on top of each steak, gently molding to the steak's shape to create a crust. Place the filets in the oven and cook for 10 minutes for medium-rare, or until to desired doneness. Garnish with the remaining 1 tablespoon parsley. ***Makes 6 servings.***

SHOPPING TIP

Beef is a favorite at Stew Leonard's.

For maximum freshness, look for meat that's bright red, cold, and firm to the touch. There should be very little "purge" or juice in the package. If the meat has bones, they should be milky white.

SIZZLING BEEF FAJITAS

¼ cup fresh lime juice

4 tablespoons olive oil, divided

3 cloves garlic, minced

1½ teaspoons ground cumin

½ teaspoon salt

½ teaspoon ground red pepper

2 pounds skirt steak

16 flour tortillas (8-inch)

3 medium red, yellow, and/or green bell peppers, cut into strips

1 large onion, cut into wedges

¼ cup chopped fresh cilantro

4 ounces shredded Monterey Jack cheese (about 1 cup)

Prepared salsa

Prepared guacamole

WINE PAIRING

Zinfandel or Syrah

GREAT ON THE GRILL

In a large zip-top plastic bag, combine the lime juice, 3 tablespoons of the oil, garlic, cumin, salt, and pepper. Add the skirt steak, seal, and turn to coat. Refrigerate for 3 to 24 hours, turning occasionally.

Thirty minutes before serving, remove the steak from the refrigerator. Preheat the grill. Wrap the tortillas in foil. Grill the steak, turning once, for 6 minutes for rare, or until an instant-read thermometer inserted in the center registers 145°F for medium-rare. Remove to a cutting board and let stand for 5 minutes. Place the foil-wrapped tortillas on the grill to warm.

Grilled skirt steak, tender and flavorful, is the base of these mouthwatering fajitas.

Meanwhile, heat the remaining 1 tablespoon oil in a large skillet over medium-high heat. Add the peppers and onion and cook, stirring frequently, for 8 minutes, or until tender and browned. Slice the meat and toss into the vegetable mixture with the cilantro. Serve with the warmed tortillas, cheese, salsa, and guacamole. ***Makes 6 to 8 servings.***

COOKING TIP

To cut an onion into wedges, cut off the stem end and remove and discard the paper skin. Place the onion stem end down and halve it. Place one half, cut side down, on a cutting board. Holding the onion at the root end, make several vertical cuts completely through the onion.

CUSTOMER RECIPE COOK-OFF

Shelley lives on Long Island during the school year and spends her summers on Candlewood Lake, near Stew Leonard's Danbury store. According to Shelley, "The second I stepped into Stew's in Danbury, I was enthralled. First, each and every person there is smiling and happy to be an employee of the store. This is reflected in their attitudes toward the customer. The freshness is remarkable, and the quality is most impressive. Since we have a house full of company each weekend, no one goes home without a trip to our favorite store. We bring carloads of food home when we are ready to come to the island once again. We cannot wait for the Farmingdale store to open; all of our friends will be the first in line."

Shelley's Steak Tuscany recipe inspires her because it reflects her favorite flavors of Italy (she has been there three times). Shelley says she has been cooking her entire married life and loves to do so.

Shelley and her husband of 27 years have three sons, two of whom have cerebral palsy. They are very involved with United Cerebral Palsy of Greater Suffolk.

SHELLEY OBLETZ'S
STEAK TUSCANY

1 sirloin steak (about 2 pounds)

1 teaspoon ground black pepper, divided

¼ cup olive oil

2 tablespoons red wine vinegar

1 clove garlic, minced

1 teaspoon kosher salt, divided

8 vine-ripened tomatoes, chopped

2 cups arugula leaves

1 medium head radicchio, thinly shredded

3 scallions, finely sliced

3 ounces Gorgonzola cheese, crumbled

Preheat the grill. Brush the grill rack with olive oil. Sprinkle the steak with ½ teaspoon of the pepper and ½ teaspoon of the salt. Grill the steak, turning once, for 25 minutes for medium-rare, or until an instant-read thermometer inserted in the center registers 145°F.

Meanwhile, in a large bowl, whisk together the oil, vinegar, garlic, and the remaining ½ teaspoon salt and ½ teaspoon pepper. Add the tomatoes, arugula, radicchio, and scallions. Toss to coat well. Add the cheese and mix gently.

Let the steak stand 10 minutes before slicing. Slice the steak against the grain. Place the slices on a platter and place the salad over the steak. ***Makes 6 to 8 servings.***

THE ULTIMATE CHEESEBURGER

1 pound ground beef

1 tablespoon Worcestershire sauce

1 large egg, lightly beaten

¼ cup seasoned bread crumbs

4 ounces Cheddar cheese, cut into ½-inch cubes

WINE PAIRING

Pinot Noir or Beaujolais

30 MINUTES OR LESS

Preheat the grill or broiler.

In a large bowl, combine the beef, Worcestershire sauce, egg, bread crumbs, and cheese. Gently mix just until blended. Shape into 4 burgers.

GREAT ON THE GRILL

Place the burgers on the grill rack or a rack in a broiler pan. Grill or broil (4 inches from the heat source) for 10 minutes, or until an instant-read thermometer inserted in the center registers 160°F. ***Makes 4 servings.***

COOKING TIP

You can make your own bread crumbs with leftover bread by placing sliced bread in a preheated 250°F oven until it's completely dry. Process it in a food processor or blender until crumbs form and store them in an airtight container in the freezer for up to 4 months.

SEVENTIES FLASHBACK SALISBURY STEAK

1 pound lean ground beef

½ small onion, finely chopped

1 tablespoon horseradish

½ teaspoon salt

¼ teaspoon ground black pepper

2 tablespoons butter

4 ounces sliced assorted mushrooms

1 cup beef broth

WINE PAIRING

Merlot, Pinot Noir, or Cabernet

30 MINUTES OR LESS

GREAT ON THE GRILL

In a medium bowl, thoroughly combine the beef, onion, horseradish, salt, and pepper. Shape into 4 oval patties.

Heat a large nonstick skillet over medium heat. Add the patties and cook, turning once, for 10 minutes, or until a thermometer inserted in the center of a patty registers 160°F. Remove to a plate and keep warm.

Add the butter to the skillet and cook until melted. Add the mushrooms and cook, stirring, for 5 minutes, or until lightly browned and all of the juices have evaporated. Add the broth and cook for 5 minutes, or until the broth is reduced by half. Return the patties to the skillet to heat through.

Makes 4 servings.

PEPPER-CUPS WITH BEEF AND RICE

2 cups crushed tomatoes, divided

¼ cup white wine

½ cup rice

¾ teaspoon salt, divided

1 pound ground beef

1 large onion, minced

1 clove garlic, minced

1 teaspoon dried thyme

1 teaspoon dried oregano

¼ teaspoon black pepper

4 medium green bell peppers

WINE PAIRING

Cabernet, Merlot, or Zinfandel

SHOPPING TIP

Selecting ground beef follows the same principles as steaks. Go for bright-red color. Meat is labeled by meat content. The more fat, thus less meat, such as 80 percent lean meat, adds juiciness to the meat and is great for hamburgers and meat loaf.

Preheat the oven to 375°F. In a 9- × 9-inch baking dish, combine ½ cup of the tomatoes and the wine. Set aside.

In a small saucepan, bring 1½ cups water to a boil over high heat. Add the rice and ¼ teaspoon of the salt. Return the water to a boil, reduce the heat to low, cover, and simmer for 20 minutes. Remove from the heat.

Meanwhile, in a large skillet over high heat, cook the beef and onion for 5 minutes. Add the garlic and cook until the beef is no longer pink.

Add the remaining 1½ cups tomatoes and the thyme, oregano, remaining ½ teaspoon salt, black pepper, and the cooked rice. Stir until well blended.

Slice off the tops of the bell peppers and remove the seeds. Divide the beef mixture among the peppers and replace the tops of the peppers. Place the peppers in the prepared baking dish. Cover the pan with foil and bake for 40 minutes, or until the beef mixture is bubbling and the peppers are tender. *Makes 4 servings.*

COOKING TIP

Cutting boards are essential to any kitchen. Select the type you like, wood or plastic, because the latest studies have shown that both are very safe.

To prevent the board from sliding around while you're cutting, place a damp paper towel under it.

Always be sure to wash the board with hot, soapy water immediately after using it to cut meats, poultry, or fish.

To remove stains from a cutting board, sprinkle the board with salt and rub with the cut side of half of a lemon.

Nothing says comfort food like meat loaf, served here with creamy mashed potatoes and green beans. Try leftovers the next day in a sandwich topped with salsa and shredded cheese.

HOME-STYLE MEAT LOAF

3 slices French bread

¼ cup milk

1 small onion, minced

1 medium red or green bell pepper, seeded and minced

1 cup ketchup, divided

1 large egg

½ teaspoon salt

¼ teaspoon black pepper

2 pounds ground beef

Cabernet or Merlot

Preheat the oven to 350°F.

Trim the crusts from the bread. Place the bread in a food processor or blender and pulse until crumbs are formed. Place the ½ cup of the bread crumbs in a large bowl and add the milk. Let sit 2 minutes, or until all of the milk is absorbed.

Add the onion, bell pepper, ½ cup of the ketchup, the egg, salt, black pepper, and beef. Using a wooden spoon or rubber spatula, blend until incorporated. Shape the mixture into a loaf and place in a baking pan. Spread the remaining ½ cup ketchup over the loaf. Bake for 1 to 1½ hours, or until an instant-read thermometer inserted in the center registers 160°F.

Let the meat loaf stand for 10 minutes before slicing. ***Makes 8 servings.***

PIZZA POT PIE

½ pound sweet Italian sausage, cut into 1-inch pieces

½ pound hot Italian sausage, cut into 1-inch pieces

2 cups marinara sauce

2 large eggs, divided

1 cup ricotta cheese

¼ cup grated Parmesan cheese

½ cup chopped parsley, divided

1 teaspoon dried oregano

¼ teaspoon freshly ground black pepper

2 cups shredded mozzarella cheese, divided

1 pound pizza dough, fresh or frozen and thawed

WINE PAIRING

Chianti or Barbera

Preheat the oven to 350°F.

In a large skillet, cook the sausage until brown. Drain well. Stir in the marinara sauce. In another bowl, combine 1 egg, the ricotta cheese, Parmesan cheese, ¼ cup of the parsley, the oregano, and pepper. Spread half of the sausage mixture into a 9- × 9-inch baking dish. Top with half of the ricotta mixture, half of the mozzarella cheese, and half of the remaining parsley. Repeat with the layers with the remaining sausage mixture, ricotta mixture, mozzarella cheese, and parsley. Roll out the pizza dough to a 10- × 10-inch square. Place the dough over the layered mixture, pinching to seal. Beat the remaining egg with 1 tablespoon water and brush top of crust. Bake for 30 minutes, or until the top is golden brown and the edges of the filling are bubbling. Let stand for 15 minutes before serving. ***Makes 6 servings.***

MEATBALLS WITH FRESH MOZZARELLA

2 tablespoons olive oil
1 clove garlic, minced
1 small onion, minced
½ pound ground pork
½ pound ground beef
½ pound ground veal
1 large egg
¼ cup milk
2 tablespoons chopped parsley
½ cup grated Parmesan cheese
½ teaspoon black pepper
¼ teaspoon salt
½ cup seasoned bread crumbs
6 ounces fresh mozzarella cheese, cut into 12 1- × 1-inch cubes

WINE PAIRING

Sangiovese or Chianti

Preheat the oven to 400°F. Lightly oil a shallow baking pan.

In a large skillet, heat the oil over medium-high heat. Add the garlic and onion and cook for 5 minutes, or until tender. Set aside.

In a large bowl, combine the pork, beef, veal, egg, milk, parsley, Parmesan cheese, pepper, salt, and bread crumbs. Add the garlic and onions. Using a wooden spoon or rubber spatula, mix until well blended. Shape the mixture into 12 balls, about 3 inches each. Make a pocket in each meatball, insert one cheese cube in the center, and reform the meatball evenly by hand. Place on the prepared pan and bake for 25 to 30 minutes, or until the meatballs are no longer pink. ***Makes 6 to 8 servings.***

SCALLOPS OF VEAL WITH ARTICHOKE HEARTS

2 tablespoons all-purpose flour

1 teaspoon salt

¼ teaspoon ground black pepper

1½ pounds veal scallops, pounded to ⅛-inch thickness

2 tablespoons butter

1 tablespoon olive oil

½ cup chicken broth

1 jar (6 ounces) marinated artichoke hearts, drained and liquid reserved

1 jar (6 ounces) roasted red peppers, drained and sliced

WINE PAIRING

Pinot Noir or Merlot

On a plate, combine the flour, salt, and pepper. Dredge the veal in the flour mixture.

Melt the butter and oil in a large skillet over medium-high heat. Working in batches, cook the veal, turning once, for 2 minutes, or until done. Remove to a plate and keep warm. Add the broth, artichoke hearts with liquid, and red peppers to the skillet. Cook, stirring to release the browned bits, for 4 minutes, or until slightly thickened. Return the veal to the skillet and cook for 1 minute, or until heated through. ***Makes 4 to 6 servings.***

This flavorful meal comes together in minutes and is elegant enough for guests. Pair the veal with hot, cooked fettuccine.

LEMON PARSLEY VEAL PICCATA

2 pounds veal cutlet

1 teaspoon salt

½ teaspoon black pepper

2 tablespoons vegetable oil

4 tablespoons butter, divided

½ cup dry white wine

½ cup chicken broth

1 clove garlic, minced

1 lemon, juiced, or more to taste
(about 2 tablespoons)

2 tablespoons capers, drained

1 tablespoon chopped parsley (optional)

WINE PAIRING

Chardonnay or Sauvignon Blanc

30 MINUTES OR LESS

Season the veal with the salt and pepper.

In a large skillet, heat the oil and 2 tablespoons of the butter over medium-high heat until the butter melts. Add a few slices of veal and cook for 3 minutes, turning once. Remove the veal to a plate and cover with foil to keep warm. Repeat with the remaining veal.

Add the wine to the skillet and cook for 4 minutes, stirring to release brown bits.

Add the broth, garlic, lemon juice, and capers and cook for 5 minutes, or until slightly thickened. Whisk in the remaining 2 tablespoons butter and the parsley until the sauce thickens. Return the veal to the skillet. Cook for 2 minutes to heat through. ***Makes 6 to 8 servings.***

VEAL MILANESE

⅓ cup all-purpose flour

1 teaspoon salt

½ teaspoon freshly ground black pepper

3 large eggs

1 cup plain bread crumbs

1 teaspoon dried basil

1 teaspoon dried thyme

2 pounds veal scaloppine, thinly sliced

2 cups vegetable oil

1 lemon, cut into 8 wedges

WINE PAIRING

**Chardonnay or
Pinot Noir**

30 MINUTES OR LESS

In a shallow bowl, combine the flour, salt, and pepper. Place the eggs in another shallow bowl and beat well. Place the bread crumbs, basil, and thyme in a third shallow bowl. Dip the veal into the flour mixture, then the eggs, and then the bread crumbs. Place the veal on a plate.

In a large skillet with high sides, heat the oil over high heat to 375°F. Carefully place 2 pieces of breaded veal in the hot oil and cook for 3 minutes, turning once. Place the cooked veal on paper towels and repeat with the remaining veal. Serve with the lemon. ***Makes 6 to 8 servings.***

VEAL SCALOPPINE WITH A TOUCH OF VINO

¼ cup all-purpose flour

1 teaspoon salt

¼ teaspoon black pepper

2 pounds boneless veal round cutlets

2 to 4 tablespoons olive oil

½ cup white wine

½ cup chicken broth

WINE PAIRING

Chianti, Chardonnay, or Pinot Grigio

30 MINUTES OR LESS

In a shallow bowl, combine the flour, salt, and pepper. Dip the veal into the flour mixture and place on a plate.

In a large skillet, heat 2 tablespoons of the oil over high heat. Working in batches, cook the veal for 3 minutes, turning once. Remove the veal to a platter and tent with foil to keep warm. Repeat with the remaining veal, adding more oil to the skillet as necessary.

Add the wine and broth to the skillet and bring to a boil, stirring to release any brown bits. Boil for 5 minutes or until reduced to about ½ cup. Pour the sauce over the veal. ***Makes 6 to 8 servings.***

SHOPPING TIP

Opt for natural broths usually sold in shelf-stable cartons. They have far less salt and better flavor than the canned ones.

VEAL CHOPS SALTIMBOCCA

4 veal rib chops, 1 inch thick (about 8 ounces each)

4 ounces Italian fontina cheese

4 slices prosciutto

½ teaspoon crumbled sage

¼ teaspoon ground black pepper

¼ teaspoon salt

WINE PAIRING

Chianti, Barbera, or Chardonnay

30 MINUTES OR LESS

GREAT ON THE GRILL

Preheat the grill or broiler.

Place the chops on a cutting board. With a sharp paring knife, horizontally cut a 2-inch-wide opening into the middle of the side of the meat. Cut a pocket in the meat, following the shape of the chop, cutting almost to the bone.

Cut the cheese into 4 pieces and wrap each in a piece of prosciutto. Insert 1 cheese stuffing piece into each chop. Sprinkle the chops with the sage and pepper.

Place the chops on the grill rack or a rack in a broiler pan. Grill or broil (4 inches from the heat source) the chops, turning once, for 13 minutes for medium doneness. Remove to a plate and sprinkle with the salt. ***Makes 4 servings.***

HERBED GRILLED VEAL CHOPS

2 tablespoons chopped fresh herbs, such as rosemary, thyme, and/or oregano

1 teaspoon citrus zest, such as orange, lemon, or lime

1 tablespoon olive oil

4 veal chops, 1 inch thick (about 8 ounces each)

½ teaspoon salt

WINE PAIRING

Cabernet, Merlot, or Côtes du Rhone

30 MINUTES OR LESS

GREAT ON THE GRILL

Preheat the grill or broiler.

In a small bowl, combine the herbs, zest, and oil. Rub over the chops. Place the chops on the grill rack or a rack in a broiler pan. Grill or broil (4 inches from the heat source) the chops, turning once, for 8 minutes, or until an instant-read thermometer inserted in the center registers 130°F. Sprinkle with the salt and serve. ***Makes 4 servings.***

COOKING TIP

Use your imagination or what you have available to prepare these flavorful chops. Some favorite combinations include cilantro and lime zest; rosemary, thyme, and orange zest; and tarragon and lemon zest.

GRILLED BUTTERFLIED LEG OF LAMB

1 small onion, finely chopped

1 clove garlic, finely minced

1 cup chili sauce

¼ cup Worcestershire sauce

¼ cup cider vinegar

1 teaspoon chili powder

1 butterflied leg of lamb
(about 3 to 4 pounds)

WINE PAIRING

**Merlot or
Pinot Noir**

GREAT
ON THE
GRILL

In a glass baking dish, combine the onion, garlic, chili sauce, Worcestershire sauce, vinegar, and chili powder. Add the lamb and turn to coat. Cover the dish with plastic wrap. Refrigerate for 4 to 48 hours, turning the lamb occasionally.

Remove the lamb from the refrigerator. Oil the grill rack and preheat the grill. Using 2 sets of tongs, lift the lamb from the marinade and place on the grill. Cook over medium heat for 40 to 60 minutes, or until an instant-read thermometer inserted in the center registers 145° for medium-rare or 160°F for medium. Turn the roast several times, brushing with the marinade only during the first 30 minutes of cooking. Discard any remaining marinade. Let stand for 10 minutes before slicing. ***Makes 8 to 12 servings.***

GEORGIA PEACH GLAZED HAM

1 bone-in smoked or cooked ham
(7 to 8 pounds)

¼ cup peach preserves

2 teaspoons Dijon mustard

2 tablespoons balsamic vinegar

WINE PAIRING

**Riesling or
dry Rosé**

Preheat the oven to 325°F.

Using a serrated knife, score the ham in a diagonal pattern. In a small bowl, stir together the preserves, mustard, and vinegar.

Place the ham on a rack in a baking dish. Roast for 2 hours (about 15 minutes per pound), or until an instant-read thermometer inserted in the center registers 120°F. Brush with the preserve mixture during the last 30 minutes of cooking. ***Makes 8 servings.***

SHOPPING TIP

Consider hams with a bone, either partially boned or bone-in because the bone contributes great flavor.

STEW LEONARD'S HAM GLAZES

Here are some of our very favorite ham glazes. Each recipe makes enough glaze for a 6- to 8-pound ham. Brush a glaze onto the baked ham during the last 30 minutes of cooking time.

1. **Apricot Glaze:** In a saucepan, heat ½ cup apricot preserves, ½ cup honey, 2 tablespoons cornstarch, 2 tablespoons lemon juice, and ¼ teaspoon ground cloves over medium-high heat. Heat and stir constantly, until thickened and bubbly. Makes 1 cup glaze.

2. **Brown Sugar Pineapple Glaze:** In a saucepan, heat 1 cup crushed pineapple in heavy syrup, ½ cup packed brown sugar, 1 tablespoon cornstarch, and 1 tablespoon Dijon mustard over medium-high heat. Heat and stir constantly, until thickened and bubbly. Makes 1½ cups glaze.

3. **Honey Glaze:** In a saucepan, heat ¼ cup packed brown sugar, 2 teaspoons cornstarch, ¼ teaspoon ground cloves or cinnamon, ½ cup honey, ½ cup pineapple juice, ¼ cup lemon juice, and 2 tablespoons Dijon mustard over medium-high heat. Heat and stir constantly, until thickened and bubbly. Makes 1½ cups glaze.

4. **Orange Apricot Glaze:** In a small bowl, combine ½ cup apricot preserves, ¼ cup orange juice, 2 tablespoons soy sauce, and 1 tablespoon lemon juice, stirring to blend well. Makes ¾ cup glaze.

5. **Peach Glaze:** In a blender, combine 1 drained can (15 ounces) peach halves in syrup, ½ cup packed brown sugar, 2 tablespoons apple cider vinegar, ½ teaspoon ground cloves, and ¼ teaspoon cinnamon. Pulse until smooth. Makes 1½ cups glaze.

6. **Traditional Pineapple Glaze:** In a blender, combine ½ cup diced fresh or crushed canned pineapple, ¼ cup packed brown sugar, ¼ cup ketchup, ¼ cup Dijon mustard, ¼ cup honey, and ⅛ teaspoon ground cloves. Pulse until smooth. Makes 1½ cups glaze.

GINGER-MARINATED PORK TENDERLOIN

¼ cup thawed frozen orange juice concentrate

3 tablespoons soy sauce

2 tablespoons toasted sesame oil

1 tablespoon grated fresh ginger

1 pork tenderloin (about 1 pound)

WINE PAIRING

Chenin Blanc or Pinot Noir

GREAT ON THE GRILL

In a zip-top plastic bag, combine the orange juice, soy sauce, oil, and ginger. Add the pork tenderloin, seal, and turn to coat. Refrigerate for 4 to 24 hours.

Preheat the grill or broiler.

Grill or broil (4 inches from the heat source) the tenderloin for 15 minutes, or until an instant-read thermometer inserted in the center registers 155°F. *Makes 4 servings.*

SHOPPING TIP

Choose pork that looks moist and is firm to the touch. Loin cuts should be pale with a hint of pink. Avoid any with yellow fat; opt for ones with pure white fat. Shoulder and leg cuts will be darker but should be selected for moist, firm meat.

TUSCAN PORK ROAST

1 pork loin roast (3 to 4 pounds)

¼ cup fresh sage leaves

3 slices prosciutto

3 medium red, yellow, and/or orange bell peppers, thinly sliced

2 medium onions, cut into wedges

1 tablespoon olive oil

½ teaspoon salt

¼ teaspoon ground black pepper

WINE PAIRING

Viognier

Preheat the oven to 350°F.

Place the roast in the center of a large roasting pan. Arrange the sage leaves over the roast. Lay the prosciutto over the sage leaves. Place the peppers and onions around the roast. Drizzle the vegetables with the oil, salt, and pepper. Toss lightly to coat.

Roast for 1¼ to 2 hours, or until an instant-read thermometer inserted in the center of the roast registers 155°F. Let stand for 10 minutes before slicing. ***Makes 8 to 10 servings.***

STORING TIP

Store pork in the refrigerator for 3 to 4 days or freeze it for up to 9 months.

PORK CHOPS WITH GRANNY SMITH APPLESAUCE

4 double-cut bone-in pork loin chops, 1½ to 2 inches thick

½ teaspoon salt

¼ teaspoon black pepper

2 tablespoons butter

2 tablespoons olive oil

4 medium Granny Smith apples, peeled, cored, and sliced

¼ cup chopped parsley

1 tablespoon fresh or 1 teaspoon dried thyme

2 tablespoons Calvados or apple-flavored liqueur

1 cup chicken broth

1 tablespoon cider vinegar

1 teaspoon sugar

Zinfandel, Pinot Noir, or a dry Riesling

SHOPPING TIP

Apples range in size and color from large and bright red to tiny and green. In between, there are many varieties available today.

Always select apples with firm, tight skin and a perceptible scent.

Preheat the oven to 375°F.

Season the pork with the salt and pepper.

In a large skillet, heat the butter and oil over medium-high heat until the butter melts. Add the pork and cook for 5 minutes, turning once, until well browned. Remove to a large roasting pan.

Add the apples, parsley, and thyme to the skillet and cook for 5 minutes, stirring frequently. Add the Calvados or liqueur and cook, stirring to break up the brown bits, for 2 minutes. Add the broth, vinegar, and sugar and cook for 5 minutes. Pour the apple mixture over the pork and bake for 30 to 40 minutes, or until an instant-read thermometer inserted in the center of a chop registers 160°F. **_Makes 4 servings._**

STORING TIP

Store apples in the refrigerator for the longest life, away from any strong-scented foods such as onions. Apples easily absorb flavors. If possible, store apples so they aren't touching each other.

THREE-HERB BREADED PORK CHOPS

¼ cup all-purpose flour

½ teaspoon salt

¼ teaspoon freshly ground black pepper

1 large egg, beaten with 1 tablespoon water

¾ cup fresh bread crumbs

¼ teaspoon dried thyme

¼ teaspoon dried marjoram

¼ teaspoon dried basil

4 bone-in, pork chops, ½ inch thick
(about 1½ pounds)

¼ cup extra-virgin olive oil

2 lemons, each cut into 6 wedges

WINE PAIRING

Chenin Blanc or Zinfandel

30 MINUTES OR LESS

In a shallow bowl, combine the flour, salt, and pepper. Place the egg and water in another shallow bowl. Place the bread crumbs, thyme, marjoram, and basil in a third shallow bowl. Dip the pork into the flour mixture, then the egg, and then the bread crumbs. Place the pork on a plate.

In a large skillet, heat the oil over medium-high heat. Add the pork and cook for 8 minutes, turning once, or until an instant-read thermometer inserted in the center of a chop registers 160°F.

Place the pork on paper towels to drain. Serve with the lemon. ***Makes 4 servings.***

BARBECUED PORK CHOPS WITH MANGO-CHILE GLAZE

½ cup red wine vinegar

¼ cup sugar

1 tablespoon fresh chiles

1 large mango, peeled and pureed

4 pork chops (about 5 ounces each)

2 tablespoons olive oil

1 teaspoon salt

WINE PAIRING

Riesling or Pinot Grigio

30 MINUTES OR LESS

GREAT ON THE GRILL

Preheat the grill or broiler.

In a small saucepan, bring the vinegar, sugar, and chiles to a boil over medium-high heat. Cook for 5 minutes, or until syrupy. Strain the chiles into a bowl. Whisk in the mango and let cool.

Brush the pork with the oil on both sides and season with the salt.

Place the pork on the grill rack or a rack in a broiler pan. Grill or broil (4 inches from the heat source) the pork, turning once, for 12 minutes, or until an instant-read thermometer inserted in the center reaches 160°F. Remove the pork from the grill and brush liberally with the glaze. ***Makes 4 servings.***

SHORT RIBS JARDINIÈRE

4 to 5 pounds short ribs

1½ teaspoons salt

½ teaspoon black pepper

2 tablespoons olive oil

2 carrots, sliced

1 large red bell pepper, diced

4 cups beef broth

¼ cup red wine

¼ cup tomato paste

2 tablespoons horseradish

1 large zucchini, sliced diagonally in half then sliced into diagonal slices

1 large yellow squash, sliced diagonally in half then sliced into diagonal slices

2 tablespoon all-purpose flour

WINE PAIRING

Pinot Noir or Merlot

Preheat the oven to 375°F.

Pat the ribs dry and sprinkle with the salt and black pepper.

In a large ovenproof pot, heat the oil over medium-high heat. Cook the ribs in batches, for 4 minutes each, or until browned on all sides. Using tongs, remove the browned ribs to a bowl. Repeat with the remaining ribs.

Add the carrots and bell pepper to the pot and cook, stirring, for 3 minutes, until browned. Add the ribs, broth, wine, tomato paste and horseradish. Bring to a boil over high heat. Transfer the pot to the oven and cook for 2 hours, or until the ribs are tender. Add the zucchini and squash and cook for 10 minutes, or until tender. Remove the pot from the oven.

Using a slotted spoon, place the ribs and vegetables in a large serving dish and cover to keep warm. Discard any loose bones.

Skim the fat from the sauce and discard the fat. Place the flour and 2 tablespoons of the sauce in a small bowl. Stir to form a paste. Bring the sauce to a boil over high heat and whisk in the flour mixture. Cook until thickened, stirring occasionally, for 3 minutes. Serve the sauce with the ribs and vegetables. *Makes 4 servings.*

SHOPPING TIP

Olive oil is an essential ingredient for fast cooking, used for salad dressings, sautéing, marinades, and more. So it's important to know the differences in grades of olive oil. Olive oil is graded for quality. In ascending order, the grades are pure, virgin, and extra-virgin. The finest oils have the least acidity.

＊ Virgin is slightly less flavorful than extra-virgin. Virgin oil is great for cooking.

＊ Extra-virgin comes entirely from the first pressing of olives and is made from premium olives with the richest aroma and flavor. Use extra-virgin for salad dressings and sauces.

＊ Pure olive oil comes from both the first and second pressings of the olives and may be blended with 5 to 10 percent virgin oil to enrich its flavor. Pure is usually sold in large cans, where it would probably go rancid prior to consumption. Avoid pure olive oils.

SWEET 'N SMOKY BABY BACK RIBS

3 racks baby back ribs (2½ to 3 pounds)

1 cup bourbon whiskey

1 tablespoon salt

1 tablespoon black pepper

1 tablespoon paprika

1 tablespoon light brown sugar

1 teaspoon garlic powder

1 teaspoon onion powder

2 cups wood chips, preferably whiskey barrel chips or hickory drained

Prepared barbecue sauce

WINE PAIRING

Riesling or Gewürztraminer

GREAT ON THE GRILL

Remove the thin papery skin from the back of each rack of the ribs or ask your butcher to do it. (Pull it off in a sheet with your fingers, using a corner of a dish towel to gain a secure grip.) Place the ribs in a roasting pan and pour the bourbon over them. Let the ribs marinate in the refrigerator for ½ hour, turning the ribs several times.

Meanwhile, in a bowl, combine the salt, pepper, paprika, brown sugar, garlic powder, and onion powder.

Pour off and discard the bourbon from the ribs. Sprinkle the ribs on both sides with two thirds of the rub, patting it in with your fingers. Let the ribs marinate for 30 minutes.

Meanwhile, preheat the grill. Set up the grill for indirect grilling and smoking, using wood chips, and adjust the heat to medium or 350°F. Arrange the ribs on a rack in the center of the grill away from the heat and cook until the ribs are very tender and the meat has pulled away from the ends of the bones, 1¼ to 1½ hours. The last 15 minutes, brush the ribs with ⅓ cup barbecue sauce. Sprinkle the ribs with the remaining rub. Serve the ribs with barbecue sauce on the side. ***Makes 4 to 6 servings.***

COOKING TIP

Grilling is a cooking method that cooks food over hot coals or another heat source such as gas. Here are some grilling tips.

❋ Always preheat your grill.

❋ Many foods, such as chicken, fish, and vegetables, turn easiest when the grill is oiled first. Using a long grill brush dipped in oil, lightly coat the grill rack.

❋ When grilling delicate foods like fish and vegetables, use two heat temperatures on the grill. For a gas grill, turn one side to high and the other to medium. For a charcoal grill, use more briquettes on the high side than the medium. Sear the foods on the high side for 1 to 2 minutes, turn and sear again. Move to the side with medium heat to finish cooking.

❋ Trim most of the fat from meat before grilling.

❋ Always allow meats to stand before carving to allow the juices to redistribute back into the meat. Individual steaks should stand for 5 minutes, and roasts should stand for 10 minutes.

❋ To boost the flavor of grilled foods, use hardwood chips. Look for them in bags with complete usage instructions.

❋ Some very handy grilling accessories include a grill basket for vegetables, a fish rack, and a set of long grill utensils.

Kathy is a Realtor with William Pitt Sotheby's International Real Estate in Newtown, Connecticut, and is also the lead singer in the band Charisma. Cooking has been a lifelong passion for Kathy, and she especially loves to cook for friends and family. She first began going to Stew Leonard's when it was just a seasonal tent on Federal Road in Danbury. Kathy is a 20-year resident of Sandy Hook, Connecticut, where she lives with her husband, Ken, and daughters, Jackie and Alyssa.

KATHY BUDA'S
BAKED GRINDER ITALIANO

3 tablespoons basil pesto

1 loaf Italian bread, sliced lengthwise

1 large tomato, thinly sliced

⅓ pound sliced provolone cheese

⅓ pound sliced deli ham

⅓ pound sliced salami

2 large fresh mozzarella balls, sliced

½ cup roasted red peppers, drained

1 jar (6.5 ounces) marinated artichoke hearts, drained

Preheat the oven to 350°F.

Spread the basil pesto on both cut sides of the bread. Layer the tomato, provolone cheese, ham, salami, and mozzarella on the bottom half of the bread. Top the cheese with the roasted peppers and artichoke hearts. Place the top half of the bread over the artichoke hearts. Completely wrap the sandwich in foil and bake for 20 minutes, or until warmed and the cheese is melted. ***Makes 6 servings.***

CHICKEN AND TURKEY

Every day in our stores around 4 p.m., we see customers scrambling around trying to figure out what to make for dinner. One of the most popular items is chicken breasts, which can be prepared quickly and easily.

At Stew Leonard's, we sell 60,000 pounds of chickens each week. Our chickens are fresh, all-natural, and hormone- and preservative-free. They're fed only the best natural feed, including fresh corn. Our chickens come from farms in Maryland and Pennsylvania. Natural chicken is becoming more and more popular at Stew Leonard's, and we're meeting this need by offering chickens by Murray's.

I think that one of the best things about chicken is its versatility. Chicken recipes range from the simplest Best-Selling Chicken Soup (page 190) to the fanciest Chicken Marsala (page 189), the Customer Cook-Off Recipe that wowed even our toughest judges. The Comforting Chicken Pot Pie (page 186) recipe is one of our stores' best sellers. My mom, Marianne Leonard, created this recipe in her own kitchen. Kids especially love it.

Close behind chicken as a family favorite is turkey. Whereas once you could buy only whole turkeys in stores, today turkey breasts, turkey cutlets, and even ground turkey are commonly available. Our customers' favorite turkey cut is turkey breast. This book features recipes for Holiday Roast Turkey with Gravy (page 214) and Turkey Scaloppine with Tomatoes and Olives (page 217). We've also included 10 Winning Ways to WOW Turkey (page 218), 10 quick and easy marinades and rubs that you can prepare to make any turkey special.

After trying out the recipes in this chapter, I hope you'll never again stand in a grocery store, looking forlornly into the chicken case and wondering what's for dinner!

10 Winning Ways to WOW

Boneless, Skinless Chicken Breasts

One of the top sellers at Stew Leonard's, chicken breasts are quick and convenient. Yet when prepared plain, they are quite boring. Here are 10 ways to turn 4 boneless, skinless chicken breast halves into flavorful, delicious meals-in-minutes. Each recipe makes 4 servings.

1. THAI CHICKEN: Heat 1 tablespoon sesame oil in a large skillet over medium-high heat. Add 4 boneless, skinless chicken breast halves and cook, turning once, for about 5 minutes, or just until browned. Remove the chicken to a plate and keep warm. To the same skillet, add 2 carrots, julienned; 1 red bell pepper, julienned; 1 onion, cut into thin wedges; and 1 clove garlic, minced. Cook for 3 minutes, or until browned. Add 1 can (14 ounces) lite coconut milk, 2 tablespoons fish sauce, and 1 to 3 teaspoons green curry paste. Return

the chicken to the skillet and bring to a simmer. Reduce the heat to low and simmer, turning the chicken once, for 10 minutes, or until an instant-read thermometer inserted in the thickest portion of the chicken registers 160°F. Stir in 2 tablespoons fresh lime juice and ¼ cup chopped fresh cilantro. Serve over jasmine, basmati, or long-grain rice.

2. FRUITED CHICKEN: On a plate, combine ⅓ cup all-purpose flour, 1 teaspoon salt, ½ teaspoon ground ginger, and ¼ teaspoon ground black pepper. Pound 4 boneless, skinless chicken breast halves to 1-inch thickness. One at a time, dredge the breasts in the flour mixture, shaking to release excess flour. Melt 2 tablespoons butter in a large skillet over medium-high heat. Cook 2 of the breasts, turning once, for 3 minutes, or until lightly browned. Remove to a plate and keep warm. Add 1 tablespoon butter to the skillet and cook the remaining 2 breasts as above. Add 1 onion, cut into wedges, for 3 minutes, or until browned. Add 3 peeled, pitted, and sliced plums. Cook for 2 minutes. Add ½ cup Madeira wine and cook, stirring, for 1 minute. Add ½ cup chicken broth and bring to a simmer. Return the chicken to the skillet, reduce the heat to low, and simmer for 5 minutes, or until an instant-read thermometer inserted in the thickest portion registers 160°F and the sauce is thickened slightly.

3. **PISTACHIO CHICKEN:** Preheat the oven to 350°F. Coat a baking sheet with non-stick cooking spray. On a plate, combine ½ cup finely chopped pistachios and ½ cup bread crumbs. In a shallow bowl, whisk together 1 egg and 1 tablespoon water. One at a time, dip 4 boneless, skinless chicken breast halves into the egg mixture and then into the pistachio mix-

ture. Place on the prepared baking sheet. Spray the breasts lightly with nonstick cooking spray and bake, turning once, for 20 minutes, or until golden brown and an instant-read thermometer inserted in the thickest portion registers 160°F.

4. **SAGE-PROSCIUTTO CHICKEN:** Preheat the oven to 350°F. Coat a baking pan with cooking spray. Place 4 boneless, skinless chicken breast halves on a work surface. Diagonally arrange 4 to 6 sage leaves over each breast half. Place a slice of prosciutto over each breast, tucking the ends under the breast. Place on the prepared pan and bake for 20 minutes, or until an instant-read thermometer inserted in the thickest portion registers 160°F.

5. **BALSAMIC CHICKEN AND ONIONS:** Season 4 boneless, skinless chicken breast halves with ½ teaspoon salt and ¼ teaspoon ground black pepper. Heat 1 tablespoon olive oil in a large skillet over medium-high heat. Cook the breasts for 5 minutes, turning once, until browned. Remove to a plate and keep warm. To the same skillet, add 2 large onions, cut into wedges, and cook, stirring, for 3 minutes, or until softened. Add 2 tablespoons balsamic vinegar and cook for 1 minute to

deglaze the pan. Add 1 cup chicken broth and bring to a boil. Return the chicken to the skillet, reduce the heat to medium-low, cover, and simmer for 10 minutes, or until an instant-read thermometer inserted in the thickest portion of the chicken registers 160°F.

6. CAPONATA CHICKEN: Season 4 boneless, skinless chicken breast halves with ½ teaspoon salt and ¼ teaspoon ground black pepper. Heat 1 tablespoon olive oil in a large skillet over medium-high heat. Cook the breasts for 5 minutes, turning once, until browned. Remove to a plate and keep warm. To the same skillet, add 2 cups (about 1 pound) prepared caponata. Bring to a simmer over medium heat. Return the chicken to the skillet, reduce the heat to medium-low, cover, and simmer for 12 minutes, or until an instant-read thermometer inserted in the thickest portion of the chicken registers 160°F.

7. QUICK COQ AU VIN: In a large saucepan over medium-high heat, cook 4 slices bacon, chopped, for 4 minutes, or until crisp. Using a slotted spoon, remove to a paper towel–lined plate. Remove all but 2 tablespoons of the drippings. To the drippings, add 2 ribs celery, chopped; 2 carrots, chopped; 2 cups sliced mushrooms; 1 clove garlic, minced; and ½ teaspoon dried thyme, crushed. Cook, stirring occasionally, until tender, about 4 minutes. Add 4 boneless, skinless chicken breast halves, cut into thin strips. Cook for 5 minutes or until browned, stirring frequently. Return the bacon to the pan with ½ cup red wine and cook for 3 minutes, stirring to release browned bits. Whisk 1 tablespoon all-purpose flour into 1 cup chicken broth. Add to the pan and cook for 5 minutes, or until thickened.

8. CHICKEN PARMESAN FINGERS: Preheat the oven to 400°F. Coat a large baking sheet with cooking spray. On a plate, combine ⅔ cup seasoned bread crumbs, ⅔ cup grated Parmesan cheese, ½ teaspoon salt, and ¼ teaspoon ground black pepper. In a pie plate, beat 1 egg with 2 tablespoons water. Cut 4 boneless, skinless chicken breast halves into 1-inch strips. Dip the strips, a few at a time, into the egg mixture then into the bread crumb mixture, pressing to coat well. Place the strips on the prepared baking sheet. Spray the strips with cooking spray. Bake for 15 minutes, or until the chicken is browned and cooked through, turning once.

9. CHICKEN WITH DRIED FRUIT: Season 4 boneless, skinless chicken breast halves with ½ teaspoon salt and ¼ teaspoon ground black pepper. Heat 1 tablespoon butter in a large skillet over medium-high heat. Cook the breasts for 5 minutes, turning once, until browned. Remove to a plate and keep warm. To the same skillet, add 1 small red onion, chopped, and cook, stirring, for 3 minutes, or until softened. Add 2 tablespoons apple cider vinegar, cooking for 1 minute to deglaze. Add 2 cups mixed dried fruit, coarsely chopped; 1 cup apple cider or juice; and 2 tablespoons brown sugar. Bring to a simmer over medium heat. Return the chicken and any accumulated juices to the skillet, reduce the heat to medium-low, cover, and simmer for 12 minutes, or until an instant-read thermometer inserted in the thickest portion of the chicken registers 160°F.

10. PESTO AND TOMATO CHICKEN: Preheat the oven to 350°F. Place 4 boneless, skinless chicken breast halves in a heavy roasting pan or cast-iron skillet. Spread 1 tablespoon prepared pesto on each. Cut 3 large tomatoes into quarters. Arrange the tomatoes around the chicken, sprinkling with a pinch of salt. Roast for 15 to 20 minutes, or until an instant-read thermometer inserted in the thickest portion of the chicken registers 160°F.

COMFORTING CHICKEN POT PIE

2 tablespoons butter

1 large onion, chopped

2 carrots, sliced

2 ribs celery, sliced

¼ cup all-purpose flour

1 cup chicken broth

½ cup white wine

1 cup half-and-half

2½ cups cooked chicken or turkey, cut into chunks

1 cup frozen peas, thawed

1 sheet refrigerated or frozen and thawed pie crust

WINE PAIRING

Chardonnay

Preheat the oven to 375°F. Grease a 3-quart baking dish.

Melt the butter in a large saucepan over medium-high heat. Add the onion, carrots, and celery and cook, stirring frequently, for 5 minutes or until tender. Add the flour and cook, stirring constantly for 2 minutes. Gradually whisk in the wine, stirring until well blended and thickened, about 4 minutes. Stir in the half-and-half, chicken, and peas. Cook over medium heat for 3 minutes, or just until simmering.

Meanwhile, roll out the pie crust on a lightly floured surface to 1-inch larger than the baking dish.

Place the chicken mixture in the prepared dish. Top with the pie crust. Crimp the crust and decorate with any remaining dough if desired. Cut 2 to 3 slices in the top to vent.

This comfort-food favorite will please both children and adults.

Place the baking pan on a baking sheet and bake for 20 to 30 minutes, or until browned and bubbling.

Let stand for 10 minutes before serving. ***Makes 4 to 6 servings.***

COOKING TIP

Substitute a variety of vegetables for the carrot and peas in this dish. Try cauliflower and broccoli, green beans and corn, or asparagus and red bell pepper.

Stew Leonard's
CUSTOMER RECIPE
COOK - OFF

Catherine has been shopping at Stew Leonard's since 1973, when she moved to Fairfield, Connecticut, from Brooklyn, New York. Her children loved coming along to visit "Stew's Little Farm." Catherine recommends Stew Leonard's to friends and neighbors and brings out-of-town relatives to Stew's when they visit.

When asked about her Chicken Marsala, Catherine says, "I started making it for my son-in-law, because he loves mushrooms. Now, whenever I cook it I get compliments."

Catherine has been married for 38 years and works as a secretary at Sacred Heart University.

CATHERINE GACCIONE'S
CHICKEN MARSALA

1 pound boneless, skinless chicken breast halves, cut into 2-inch strips

2 tablespoons all-purpose flour

½ teaspoon salt

¼ teaspoon ground black pepper

1 tablespoon olive oil

1 tablespoon butter

1 pound mushrooms, sliced

4 shallots, sliced

1 clove garlic, minced

1 cup Marsala wine

1 tablespoon tomato paste

1 can (14 ounces) chicken broth

In a zip-top plastic bag, combine the chicken, flour, salt, and pepper. Seal and shake to coat the chicken.

Heat the oil and butter in a large skillet over medium-high heat. Add the chicken and cook, turning frequently, for 4 minutes, or until cooked through and golden brown. Remove the chicken to a plate and keep warm.

Add the mushrooms, shallots, and garlic and cook, stirring, for 3 minutes, or until browned. Add the Marsala and cook, stirring, for 1 minute. Add the tomato paste and broth and bring to a simmer. Add the chicken. Reduce the heat to low, cover, and cook for 10 minutes. **Makes 4 servings.**

BEST-SELLING CHICKEN SOUP

2 tablespoons olive oil

1 medium red onion, chopped

2 ribs celery, chopped

2 large carrots, chopped

1 clove garlic, minced

4 cups chicken broth

1 pound boneless, skinless chicken breasts, cut into 1-inch cubes

1 cup bow-tie, shell, or rotelle pasta

2 tablespoons fresh chopped dillweed or 2 teaspoons dried

1 cup frozen peas, thawed

¼ cup grated Parmesan or Romano cheese (optional)

WINE PAIRING

Chardonnay or Sauvignon Blanc

30 MINUTES OR LESS

Heat the oil in a large saucepan over medium-high heat. Add the onion, celery, carrots, and garlic and cook, stirring frequently, for 5 minutes until tender. Add the broth and 4 cups water and bring to a boil. Stir in the chicken, pasta, and dill. Cook for 5 minutes, or until the chicken is cooked through. Stir in the peas and cook for 1 minute. Serve in bowls and sprinkle the tops with 2 teaspoons of the cheese if using. ***Makes 6 servings.***

BEER CAN CHICKEN

1 can beer or ginger ale

1 medium onion, cut into wedges

3 cloves garlic, minced

1 recipe Southwest Rub (see page 213)

1 whole chicken (about 3½ pounds)

WINE PAIRING

Sauvignon Blanc or Chardonnay

GREAT ON THE GRILL

Preheat the grill.

Using a can opener, remove the entire top of the beer or soda can. Pour half of the can into an ice-cold glass and enjoy while preparing the meal. Add the onion, garlic, and about ⅓ of the spice rub mixture into the can. Place the can in an aluminum drip pan. Holding a leg in each hand, place the large cavity of the bird over the can. (You may want to get assistance holding the can.)

Place the aluminum pan holding the can and bird on the grill. Grill the chicken over indirect heat for 1¼ hours, or until an instant-read thermometer inserted in a breast reaches 180°F. ***Makes 4 to 6 servings.***

COOKING TIP

This cooking technique is so popular these days, it was important to include it here. Many "grill masters" will delight in learning it. Basically, the chicken will stand on the can of beer while it cooks. The evaporating beer will flavor the chicken while it grills. You may substitute any of the rubs on pages 212 and 213 for the Southwest Rub.

HUNTER-STYLE CHICKEN CACCIATORE

1 whole chicken (about 3½ pounds),
cut into 8 pieces

½ teaspoon salt

¼ teaspoon ground black pepper

2 tablespoons olive oil

8 cloves garlic, peeled

8 ounces button mushrooms, quartered

1 large onion, chopped

1 large green bell pepper, chopped

1 teaspoon dried basil

½ teaspoon fennel seeds

¼ cup dry red wine

1 can (28 ounces) whole tomatoes in juice

½ can (6 ounces) tomato paste

1 tablespoon sugar

WINE PAIRING

Chianti

Sprinkle the chicken with the salt and black pepper.

Heat the oil in a large saucepot or skillet over medium-high heat. Add the chicken and cook until browned, about 5 minutes, turning to brown all sides. Place the chicken on a plate.

Add the garlic, mushrooms, onion, bell pepper, basil, and fennel seeds to the same skillet and cook, stirring frequently, for 5 minutes. Add the

A favorite among Italian dishes, cacciatore means "hunter" in Italian. This dish is prepared hunter-style with tomatoes, onion, mushrooms, and herbs.

wine to deglaze. Stir in the tomatoes, tomato paste, and sugar and bring to a boil. Add the chicken. Reduce the heat to low, cover, and simmer for 25 minutes, or until an instant-read thermometer inserted in the thickest portion of the chicken registers 170°F. **Makes 6 to 8 servings.**

SHOPPING TIP

When you select whole chickens, broilers are the smallest type at less than 2½ pounds. Roasters are the largest at about 4½ pounds, and fryers are between the two.

CHICKEN ROULADE

4 boneless, skinless chicken breast halves

1 teaspoon salt, divided

½ teaspoon black pepper, divided

1 cup baby spinach

4 large pieces roasted red peppers

2 slices (¼ inch each) fresh mozzarella cheese, cut lengthwise in half

2 portabello mushrooms, sliced

¼ cup all-purpose flour

3 tablespoons olive oil

WINE PAIRING

Côtes du Rhone or Chardonnay

Place the chicken on a cutting board. With a paring knife held parallel to the surface, cut into the center of a breast almost to the edge, but leaving one side intact. Open the breast like a book. Repeat with all of the breasts. Sprinkle the chicken with ½ teaspoon of the salt and ¼ teaspoon of the pepper.

Evenly divide the spinach, red pepper, cheese, and mushrooms between the chicken, forming thin layers of each over the breasts. Starting from one long side, roll the breasts, jelly-roll style. Secure with toothpicks or string. Cover and refrigerate for 1 to 8 hours.

Preheat the oven to 350°F.

In a shallow bowl, combine the flour and the remaining salt and pepper. Dredge the chicken rolls in the flour mixture.

In a large skillet, heat the oil over medium-high heat. Add the rolls and cook, turning, until browned on all sides. Place on a baking pan. Bake for 15 minutes, or until an instant-read thermometer inserted in the thickest portion of meat registers 160°F. ***Makes 4 servings.***

MY DAUGHTER BLAKE'S CHICKEN

1 lemon

¼ cup olive oil

¼ cup white wine

2 cloves garlic, minced

1 tablespoon fresh sage, chopped

1 teaspoon salt

½ teaspoon black pepper

1 whole chicken (about 4 pounds)

WINE PAIRING

**Merlot or
Sauvignon Blanc**

From the lemon, grate 1 teaspoon of the zest and squeeze ¼ cup juice. Place the zest and juice in a large bowl along with the oil, wine, garlic, sage, salt, and pepper. Add the chicken and turn to coat. Leaving the chicken breast side down, loosely cover the bowl and let stand for 1 hour, occasionally basting with the marinade.

Preheat the oven to 375°F.

Remove the chicken from the marinade and place on a rack in a roasting pan. Bake for the chicken for 1¼ hours, or until an instant-read thermometer inserted in the thickest portion of meat registers 180°F. ***Makes 6 servings.***

BROCCOLI-CHICKEN STIR FRY

1 cup chicken broth

2 tablespoons soy sauce

1 tablespoon cornstarch

2 to 4 tablespoons sesame oil

2 boneless, skinless chicken breast halves, cut into thin strips

1 medium onion, cut into thin wedges

1 medium red or yellow bell pepper, cut into thin strips

4 cups broccoli florets

½ can sliced water chestnuts

1 tablespoon minced ginger

1 clove garlic, minced

1 chopped scallion, for garnish

2 cups cooked jasmine rice

WINE PAIRING

Riesling or Viognier

30 MINUTES OR LESS

COOKING TIP

Julienne strips are long, narrow strips of food, usually vegetables.

To cut julienne strips, cut the food into 2-inch pieces. Make several parallel cuts in each piece.

Stack the pieces and cut crosswise to form strips.

In a small measuring cup, whisk together the broth, soy sauce, and cornstarch. Set aside.

Heat 2 tablespoons of the oil in a wok or large skillet over high heat. Add the chicken and cook for 5 minutes, stirring constantly, or until browned. With a slotted spoon, remove the chicken to a plate and cover.

Add the remaining 2 tablespoons oil to the skillet if necessary. Add the onion, pepper, and broccoli and cook for 4 minutes, stirring constantly. Add the water chestnuts, ginger, and garlic and cook 1 minute, or until the vegetables are tender-crisp. Whisk the broth mixture and add to the wok or skillet. Return the chicken and any juices to the wok. Cook, stirring constantly, until the sauce is thickened. Garnish with the scallion and serve over the rice. ***Makes 4 servings.***

STORING TIP

Store chicken in its packaging at the back of your refrigerator's bottom shelf for up to 2 days.

CHICKEN ENCHILADAS

1 clove garlic, minced

2 tablespoons soy sauce

1 tablespoon lime juice

½ teaspoon ground coriander

½ teaspoon ground cumin

¼ teaspoon salt

¼ teaspoon ground black pepper

1 pound boneless, skinless chicken breasts

2 tablespoons olive oil

2 medium red and/or green bell peppers, thinly sliced

1 medium red onion, thinly sliced

8 flour tortillas (8-inch) or four 12-inch tortillas

Prepared salsa

Prepared guacamole

Sour cream

WINE PAIRING

Syrah

GREAT ON THE GRILL

In a zip-top plastic bag, combine the garlic, soy sauce, lime juice, coriander, cumin, salt, and black pepper. Add the chicken breasts, seal, and turn to coat. Refrigerate for 4 to 8 hours.

Preheat the grill or broiler. Remove the chicken breasts from the marinade and place on an oiled grill rack or a rack in a broiler pan. Grill or broil (4 inches from the heat source) for 15 minutes, or until an instant-read thermometer inserted in the thickest portion reaches 160°F.

Meanwhile, heat the oil in a large skillet over medium-high heat. Add the bell peppers and onion and cook for 8 minutes, or until tender and browned.

Cut the chicken on the bias into ½-inch strips. Serve with the onion mixture, tortillas, salsa, guacamole, and sour cream. To eat, fill a tortilla with some of the chicken, onion mixture, salsa, guacamole, and sour cream. Roll and eat. **Makes 4 servings.**

COOKING TIP

Cook boneless chicken breasts and thighs to 160°F. Chicken breasts, legs, and thighs with bones should reach 170°F. Cook whole chickens to 180°F.

ROSEMARY ROASTED CHICKEN

2 tablespoons olive oil

2 tablespoons fresh chopped rosemary

2 cloves garlic, minced

Pinch chili pepper flakes

1 teaspoon salt

½ teaspoon black pepper

1 whole roasting chicken (5 to 7 pounds)

WINE PAIRING

Chardonnay or dry Rosé

Preheat the oven to 375°F.

In a small bowl, combine the oil, rosemary, garlic, chili pepper, salt, and black pepper. Rub the mixture around the chicken, making sure the cavity gets seasoned too.

Bake the chicken for 1¾ to 2¼ hours, or until an instant-read thermometer inserted in the thickest portion registers 180°F. Remove the chicken to a cutting board and let rest for 10 minutes before slicing. *Makes 6 to 8 servings.*

COOKING TIP

Herbs, such as rosemary, add much flavor and variety to dishes.

The fastest way to chop a bunch of fresh herbs is with scissors. Place the herbs in a small cup and snip them until they are finely chopped.

ORCHARD APPLE CIDER CHICKEN

¼ cup all-purpose flour

½ teaspoon salt

¼ teaspoon black pepper

4 boneless, skinless chicken breast halves

3 tablespoons butter, divided

3 Granny Smith apples, peeled, cored, and thickly sliced

¼ cup finely chopped shallots

1 tablespoon fresh or 1 teaspoon dried thyme

½ cup apple cider

½ cup chicken broth

3 teaspoons cream

1 tablespoon fresh chopped parsley

WINE PAIRING

Viognier

In a large shallow bowl, combine the flour, salt, and pepper. Dredge the chicken in the flour mixture. In a large skillet, melt 2 tablespoons of the butter over medium-high heat. Add the chicken and cook for 5 minutes, turning once, or until well browned. Transfer the chicken to a plate and tent with foil. Add the remaining 1 tablespoon butter to the skillet. Once melted, add the apples, shallots, and thyme. Cook, stirring, for 5 minutes, or until lightly browned. Add the apple cider and broth and bring to a simmer. Return the chicken and juices to the skillet and reduce the heat to low. Cover and simmer until the chicken is cooked through, about 10 minutes.

Place the chicken on a warmed platter and stir the cream and parsley into the sauce. Spoon the sauce over the chicken. ***Makes 4 servings.***

CHEF ART'S CHICKEN MARGARITA

¼ cup all-purpose flour

½ teaspoon salt

¼ teaspoon black pepper

4 boneless, skinless chicken breast halves

2 tablespoons virgin olive oil

1 clove garlic, minced

½ cup crushed tomatoes

¼ cup white wine

¼ cup chicken broth

1 tablespoon fresh or 1 teaspoon dried sage

1 tablespoon fresh or 1 teaspoon dried parsley

2 thin slices ham, cut crosswise in half

4 thin slices cut from a large tomato

4 thin slices fresh mozzarella cheese

WINE PAIRING

Chianti or Barbera

30 MINUTES OR LESS

COOKING TIP

An egg slicer works great for cutting mozzarella cheese into uniform slices.

In a large shallow bowl, combine the flour, salt, and pepper. Dredge the chicken in the flour mixture.

In a large skillet, heat the oil over medium-high heat. Add the garlic and cook for 1 minute, until lightly brown. Add the chicken and cook for 5 minutes, turning once, until lightly browned.

Add the crushed tomatoes, wine, broth, sage, parsley, and any remaining flour mixture. Stir until well blended. Bring to a simmer, cover, and simmer for 5 minutes. Carefully top each chicken breast with a slice of the ham, tomato, and cheese, cover, and simmer for 3 minutes, or until an instant-read thermometer inserted in the thickest portion of the chicken registers 160°F. ***Makes 4 servings.***

SHOPPING TIP

To freeze chicken, place it in zip-top freezer bags, date it, and place it in the back of the freezer. Keep it for up to 2 months. If you have more than one freezer, store meat in the one that is opened less so it remains at a constant temperature.

ARROZ CON POLLO

4 skinless chicken thighs

4 chicken drumsticks

½ teaspoon salt, divided

¼ teaspoon ground black pepper, divided

2 tablespoons olive oil

2 carrots, sliced

2 ribs celery, sliced

1 medium onion, thinly sliced

1 tablespoon chopped fresh thyme
or 1 teaspoon dried thyme

2 cups chicken broth

1 cup prepared salsa

1 teaspoon hot-pepper sauce

1 cup rice

2 cups frozen peas, thawed

WINE PAIRING

**Chardonnay or
dry Rosé**

Sprinkle the chicken with ¼ teaspoon of the salt and ⅛ teaspoon of the pepper.

Heat the oil in a large saucepan over medium-high heat. Cook the chicken for 10 minutes, or until browned. Remove to a plate and keep warm. To the saucepan, add the carrots, celery, onion, thyme, the remaining ¼ teaspoon salt, and the remaining ⅛ teaspoon pepper. Cook, stirring occasionally, for 5 minutes, or until tender-crisp. Add the broth, salsa, and hot-pepper sauce. Bring to a boil over high heat. Stir in the rice and add the chicken. Reduce the heat to low, cover, and simmer for 20 minutes, or until the rice is tender and an instant-read thermometer inserted in the thickest portion of the chicken registers 170°F. Stir in the peas and cook for 1 minute. ***Makes 4 to 6 servings.***

Literally "rice with chicken," this Spanish-influenced dish makes for a hearty meal. Serve with a salad, and dinner's ready!

OVEN-FRIED CHICKEN

½ cup cornmeal

½ cup seasoned bread crumbs

½ teaspoon salt

¼ teaspoon ground black pepper

1 cup buttermilk

1 whole chicken (about 3½ pounds), cut up

WINE PAIRING

**Bordeaux,
Côtes du Rhone,
or Chardonnay**

Preheat the oven to 400°F.

In a pie plate or shallow bowl, combine the cornmeal, bread crumbs, salt, and pepper. Place the buttermilk in another pie plate or shallow bowl.

Dip the chicken pieces into the buttermilk and then into the bread crumb mixture, pressing to adhere. Place on a baking sheet. Lightly spray the chicken pieces with olive oil cooking spray.

Bake for 35 minutes, or until an instant-read thermometer inserted in the center of a breast reaches 170°F. ***Makes 6 to 8 servings.***

STORING TIP

Thaw frozen chicken on a plate in the refrigerator. For fast thawing, place it in a bowl of cold water.

CHEF CHAZ'S GORGONZOLA CHICKEN

2 tablespoons olive oil

1 tablespoon paprika

½ teaspoon salt

¼ teaspoon white pepper

4 boneless chicken breast halves

4 ounces Gorgonzola cheese

½ cup walnuts, chopped

4 scallions, chopped

WINE PAIRING

Cabernet or red Bordeaux

30 MINUTES OR LESS

Preheat the oven to 375°F.

In a small bowl, combine the oil, paprika, salt, and pepper. Place the chicken on a baking pan and coat with the paprika mixture. Bake for 15 minutes.

Meanwhile, in another bowl, combine the cheese, walnuts, and scallions.

Top each piece of chicken with a quarter of the cheese mixture and bake for another 10 minutes, or until lightly browned and an instant-read thermometer inserted in the thickest portion registers 160°F. **Makes 4 servings.**

STORING TIP

Store scallions in a zip-top plastic bag in the refrigerator for up to 1 week. Wash just before using.

THREE-BEAN CHICKEN CHILI

2 tablespoons olive oil

1 large onion, diced

1 large red bell pepper, diced

2 cloves garlic, minced

1½ pounds ground chicken, preferably thigh meat

1 can (28 ounces) crushed tomatoes

1 tablespoon light chili powder

1 tablespoon sugar

1 teaspoon cumin

1 teaspoon chipotle paste

1 teaspoon salt

½ teaspoon black pepper

1 cup chicken broth

1 can (15 ounces) small white beans, rinsed and drained

1 can (15 ounces) pinto beans, rinsed and drained

1 can (15 ounces) black beans, rinsed and drained

1½ cup corn kernels, fresh or frozen and thawed

¼ cup fresh chopped cilantro

WINE PAIRING

Riesling

In a stockpot, heat the oil over medium-high heat. Add the onion and bell pepper and cook for 5 minutes. Add the garlic and cook for 2 minutes. Add the chicken and cook well, stirring occasionally, until the chicken is no longer pink.

Add the tomatoes, chili powder, sugar, cumin, chipotle paste, salt, and black pepper. Stir to mix well and cook for 10 minutes. Add the broth and bring to a simmer. Reduce the heat to low, cover, and cook for 30 minutes. Add the white beans, pinto beans, and black beans and cook for 15 minutes, or until the flavors are well blended. Stir in the corn and cilantro and cook for 2 minutes. ***Makes 12 servings.***

COOKING TIP

Beans are a great source of fiber and vegetarian protein. Canned beans are a healthful fast food.

Beans are preserved in cans with salt added. To remove about ⅓ of this added salt, always rinse beans before using. This also brings out their unique flavor.

STEW'S AWARD-WINNING SANTA FE CHICKEN PIZZA

1 loaf (1 pound) prepared pizza dough, thawed if frozen

2 tablespoons olive oil

1 clove garlic, minced

1 teaspoon chili powder

1 teaspoon paprika

½ teaspoon salt

¼ teaspoon black pepper

Pinch ground red pepper

2 boneless chicken breast halves

½ cup prepared salsa

½ cup jarred marinara sauce

½ cup roasted red peppers, drained

¾ cup shredded mozzarella cheese

¾ cup shredded Cheddar cheese

WINE PAIRING

Riesling or Beaujolais

GREAT ON THE GRILL

SHOPPING TIP

Pizza dough or bread dough is available already prepared in the refrigerator section of stores. Use it for homemade pizza, calzones, or home-baked bread.

Allow the pizza dough to rise according to the package directions.

In a large zip-top plastic bag, combine the oil, garlic, chili powder, paprika, salt, black pepper, and red pepper. Add the chicken, turning to coat. Seal the bag and allow the chicken to marinate on the counter for 30 minutes.

Preheat the grill or broiler. Grill or broil the chicken for 20 minutes, or until an instant-read thermometer inserted in the thickest portion registers 160°F. Let the chicken sit for 10 minutes. Cut the chicken into ½-inch slices.

Preheat the oven to 375°F.

In a small bowl, combine the salsa and marinara sauce.

On a lightly floured surface, roll the dough to a 12-inch circle and place on a pizza pan or baking sheet. Top the dough with the sauce, chicken slices, red peppers, mozzarella cheese, and Cheddar cheese.

Bake according to the pizza dough package directions, or until the dough has risen and lightly browned. ***Makes 8 slices.***

COOKING TIP

To grill the pizza instead, after you roll out the dough, coat the preheated grill with oil. Place the dough round on the grill. Cook for 2 to 3 minutes, or until the top bubbles slightly. Using tongs, turn the dough and cook for 1 to 2 minutes longer, or until lightly browned. Remove to a baking sheet. Top the dough with the sauce, chicken slices, red peppers, mozzarella cheese, and Cheddar cheese. Using a metal spatula, slide the pizza back on the grill. Cook for 1 minute longer to melt the cheese.

10 Winning Ways to WOW

Marinades and Rubs

Adding flavor to meats and poultry is as easy as preparing one of these marinades or rubs. The recipes make enough for 4 chicken breasts, 1 steak, 1 pork tenderloin, or 4 pork chops. Prepare the marinades in a bowl or a zip-top plastic bag. Add the poultry or meat and refrigerate. For the rubs, combine the ingredients in a small bowl and rub over the meat. It's best to marinate chicken breasts for 2 to 4 hours. Steak and pork can marinate for up to 24 hours.

1. SANTA FE MARINADE: In a bowl, combine ½ cup buttermilk, 2 tablespoons fresh lime juice, 2 tablespoons chopped fresh cilantro, and 1 clove garlic, minced.

2. HONEY-MUSTARD MARINADE: In a bowl, whisk together 2 tablespoons honey mustard and 2 tablespoons balsamic vinegar. Whisk in 2 tablespoons olive oil.

3. CITRUS-ROSEMARY MARINADE: In a bowl, whisk together 3 tablespoons orange juice; 1 tablespoon chopped fresh rosemary or 1 teaspoon dried rosemary; 1 clove garlic, minced; and ¼ teaspoon ground black pepper. Whisk in 2 tablespoons olive oil.

4. PESTO MARINADE: In a bowl, whisk together ⅓ cup prepared pesto and 2 tablespoons white balsamic vinegar.

5. SESAME-SOY MARINADE: In a bowl, whisk together ¼ cup rice wine vinegar, 2 tablespoons soy sauce, 2 tablespoons toasted sesame oil, 1 tablespoon fresh grated ginger or 1 teaspoon ground ginger, and ¼ teaspoon crushed red pepper.

6. CURRY MARINADE: In a bowl, whisk together ¼ cup plain yogurt, 1 tablespoon curry powder, 1 tablespoon chopped fresh cilantro, ½ teaspoon ground coriander, ½ teaspoon ground cumin, and ¼ teaspoon ground ginger.

7. SOUTHWEST RUB: In a small bowl, stir together 1 teaspoon lime zest, 1 teaspoon chili powder, 1 teaspoon salt, ½ teaspoon ground cumin, ½ teaspoon dried crushed oregano, and 1 clove garlic, minced.

8. PROVENCE RUB: In a small bowl, stir together 2 tablespoons olive oil, 4 pitted black olives such as niçoise or calamata, 1 tablespoon dried herbes de Provence, and 1 clove garlic, minced.

9. CHINESE FIVE-SPICE RUB: In a small bowl, stir together 2 tablespoons Chinese five-spice powder, 1 tablespoon brown sugar, and 1 teaspoon salt.

10. DEVILED RUB: In a small bowl, stir together 1 tablespoon paprika, 1 tablespoon brown sugar, 1 teaspoon dried crushed thyme, 1 teaspoon salt, and ¼ to ½ teaspoon ground red pepper.

HOLIDAY ROAST TURKEY WITH GRAVY

2 tablespoons chopped fresh rosemary or 2 teaspoons crushed dried rosemary

2 tablespoons orange zest

2 cloves garlic, minced

1½ teaspoons salt, divided

1 teaspoon ground black pepper, divided

1 tablespoon olive oil, divided

1 fresh turkey (about 16 pounds), rinsed and patted dry

2 medium onions, quartered

2 sprigs fresh rosemary

1½ cups chicken broth

¼ cup all-purpose flour

1 tablespoon balsamic vinegar

Rosemary sprigs for garnish

Orange peel for grarnish

WINE PAIRING

Pinot Noir or Zinfandel

Preheat the oven to 325°F.

In a small bowl, combine the rosemary, orange zest, garlic, 1 teaspoon of the salt, and ½ teaspoon of the pepper. Stir in about ½ of the oil.

Loosen the skin on the breast and legs of the turkey. Rub the orange zest mixture under the skin. Rub the remaining oil over the turkey skin. Place the onion and rosemary sprigs in the cavity of the turkey.

Place the turkey on a rack in a large roasting pan and bake for 3 to 4 hours, or until an instant-read thermometer inserted into the thickest part

The centerpiece of holiday meals, this bird tastes as good as it looks.

of the thigh, not touching the bone, registers 180°F. Loosely cover the breast with foil if the turkey browns too much during cooking.

Place the turkey on a cutting board and let stand for 20 minutes.

Meanwhile, pour the drippings from the pan into a large fat separator or measuring cup. Skim off and discard the fat. Add enough of the chicken broth to the drippings to equal 2½ cups. Place the roasting pan over 2 burners set on medium heat and stir the flour into the pan. Cook, stirring constantly, for 2 minutes. Gradually whisk the broth mixture into the pan. Cook for 3 to 5 minutes, or until thickened. Stir in the vinegar and remaining ½ teaspoon salt and the remaining ½ teaspoon pepper.

Carve the turkey and serve with the gravy. Garnish with the rosemary and orange peel. *Makes 14 to 16 servings.*

COOKING TIP

Change the herbs and seasoning of the spice rub for a variety of flavorful roasts. Substitute thyme, lemon zest, and chives for a fresh flavor; cilantro, cumin, and ginger for an Asian flair; or sage, a pinch of nutmeg, and shallots for a taste of the harvest.

Ready in just minutes, turkey cutlets are bursting with flavor when topped with olives and tomatoes. Here they're paired with Buttery Broccoli with Toasted Pine Nuts (page 81).

TURKEY SCALOPPINE WITH TOMATOES AND OLIVES

½ cup grated Parmesan cheese

¼ teaspoon salt

¼ teaspoon ground black pepper

1 pound turkey cutlets for scaloppine

2 tablespoons extra-virgin olive oil

1 pint cherry tomatoes, halved

¼ cup calamata olives, pitted and quartered

1 tablespoon fresh chopped thyme

¼ cup white wine

WINE PAIRING

Pinot Grigio

30 MINUTES OR LESS

On a plate, combine the cheese, salt, and pepper. Dredge the turkey in the cheese mixture.

Heat the oil in a large skillet over medium-high heat. Add the turkey and cook, turning once, for 4 minutes, or until no longer pink. Remove to a serving plate; keep warm.

Add the tomatoes, olives, and thyme to the skillet and cook, stirring constantly, for 2 minutes. Add the wine and cook for 2 minutes more, stirring to break up the browned bits. Place the tomato mixture over the turkey and serve. ***Makes 4 servings.***

10 Winning Ways to WOW

Turkey

Try these delicious Stew Leonard's marinades for turkey. They're simple to use. Just remove the parts from a whole turkey (a breast would work well also). Rinse the bird and place it in a large bowl or roasting pan. Pour some of the marinade into the cavity of the bird. Pour the rest over it. Cover and refrigerate overnight, turning the turkey occasionally. The next morning, remove the turkey from the marinade, discarding the marinade. Then prepare the turkey as usual.

1. WHITE WINE MARINADE: Combine 1½ cups white wine, ½ cup olive oil, 1 tablespoon herbes de Provence, 2 cloves minced garlic, 1 teaspoon salt, and ½ teaspoon black pepper.

2. INDIAN-STYLE MARINADE. Combine 2 cups yogurt, 2 tablespoons lemon juice, 2 cloves minced garlic, 1 teaspoon ground ginger, 1 teaspoon ground coriander, 1 teaspoon cumin, 1 teaspoon paprika, 1 teaspoon salt, ½ teaspoon black pepper, and ¼ teaspoon cayenne pepper.

3. HERBS MARINADE. Combine 1 cup olive oil, 1 tablespoon fresh chopped sage, 1 tablespoon fresh chopped thyme, 1 tablespoon fresh chopped rosemary, 1 crushed bay leaf, 1 teaspoon salt, and ½ teaspoon black pepper.

4. OLD-FASHIONED MUSTARD MARINADE. Combine 1½ cups white wine, ½ cup olive oil, 1 tablespoon dried mustard, 1 teaspoon salt, and ½ teaspoon black pepper.

5. CIDER MARINADE: Combine 1½ cups apple cider, ½ cup Calvodos or apple brandy, ¼ cup minced carrot, ¼ cup minced celery, 2 cloves minced garlic, 1 teaspoon salt, and ½ teaspoon black pepper.

6. TWO VINEGAR MARINADE: Combine ½ cup olive oil, ½ cup sherry vinegar, ½ cup red wine vinegar, 2 tablespoons Dijon mustard, 3 minced shallots, 1 tablespoon fresh chopped thyme, 1 tablespoon fresh chopped tarragon, 1 tablespoon fresh chopped chive, 1 crushed bay leaf, 1 teaspoon salt, and ½ teaspoon black pepper.

7. HERB AND BLACK OLIVE MARINADE: Combine 1 cup olive oil, ½ cup Cognac, ¼ cup minced pitted black calamata olives, 1 tablespoon fresh chopped thyme, 1 tablespoon fresh chopped rosemary, 1 crushed bay leaf, 1 teaspoon salt, and ½ teaspoon black pepper.

8. TWO CITRUS MARINADE: Combine ½ cup olive oil, ½ cup fresh squeezed lime juice, ½ cup fresh squeezed lemon juice, 2 tablespoons whisky, 2 tablespoons honey, 1 minced small onion, 1 teaspoon ground cloves, 1 teaspoon ground nutmeg, 1 teaspoon ground coriander, 1 teaspoon salt, ½ teaspoon ground ginger, ½ teaspoon freshly ground black pepper, and ¼ teaspoon ground red pepper.

9. PALE ALE MARINADE: Combine 24 ounces pale ale, ½ cup olive oil, 2 minced carrots, 2 minced ribs celery, 1 minced onion, 1 tablespoon fresh chopped thyme, 1 crushed bay leaf, 1 teaspoon salt, and ½ teaspoon black pepper.

10. ASSORTED SPICES MARINADE: Combine 2 cups yogurt, ¼ cup olive oil, 2 tablespoons ketchup, 2 cloves minced garlic, 1 teaspoon ground coriander, 1 teaspoon cumin, 1 teaspoon salt, and 1 teaspoon freshly ground peppercorn mixture.

A TIME FOR THANKSGIVING

Among dozens of family traditions in the Leonard house, one of my favorites is that almost every Thanksgiving, we experiment with a new roasted turkey recipe. Because there are so many savory ways to prepare a turkey, we like to try out new ones. You'll find one of my favorites, Holiday Roast Turkey with Gravy, on page 214.

But before you roast a great turkey, you need to buy a great turkey. At Stew Leonard's, our turkeys come from farms in the Shenandoah Valley. We visit the farmers often and inspect their operations. Our turkeys' diet—a special blend of corn, soy, and other natural feed—is closely monitored by a nutritionist to make sure the turkeys are tender and juicy. Our turkeys are all natural; they receive no artificial additives, hormones, or preservatives. Each holiday season, Stew Leonard's sells 40,000 turkeys or approximately 600,000 pounds of turkey.

The average Thanksgiving turkey is 15 pounds. When you choose *your* turkey, size does matter. Figure on 1 pound of uncooked turkey per guest. (It never hurts to overestimate, though! After-Thanksgiving turkey sandwiches are a tasty tradition.) However, it's a myth that a small turkey is more tender than a larger one. Most turkeys today are raised with similar feed and under similar conditions. Their flavor and texture are more or less the same if cooked properly.

Though both fresh and frozen turkeys are available, I recommend buying fresh turkeys over frozen ones when possible. Fresh turkeys tend to retain more of their natural juices and therefore are more tender. If you do buy a fresh turkey, it will last for 2 to 3 days in your refrigerator. Store it on the bottom shelf, which is the coldest spot in your refrigerator.

When you cook your turkey, a general rule is 15 to 18 minutes per pound in a 325°F oven, or until the internal temperature reaches 180°F. For a 15-pound turkey, that translates to 3¾ to 4½ hours. Basting the turkey while it roasts is not essential, but it does give the skin a nice golden color. If desired, baste roughly every 30 minutes during the last 2 hours of cooking.

Our Stew Leonard's chefs do not recommend stuffing your turkey. This has become a major question among our customers because of food safety. By the time the inside of your stuffed turkey reaches a temperature of 180°F, the outside of your turkey will be overcooked. To be on the safe side, always cook and serve your stuffing separately.

I'm proud to say that each year, Stew Leonard's donates thousands of turkeys to community organizations, continuing a holiday tradition that started more than 20 years ago. The organizations include church and civic groups, elderly housing and senior nutrition programs, schools, and police and fire departments, and go toward food baskets and community Thanksgiving meals.

If you live in the area, Stew Leonard's Catering offers a complete Thanksgiving dinner for eight people, including a freshly roasted marinated turkey, gravy, stuffing, potatoes, string beans almondine, cranberry orange sauce, 12 dinner rolls, and choice of pie for a great price. The meal can even be delivered to your door.

Many of our customers ask Stew Leonard's Wine Shops their picks for the best wines to serve with a Thanksgiving meal. Here are some of our favorites. Turkey is very wine friendly with neutral flavors.

Beaujolais Nouveau and Zinfandel are the two most popular wine pairings for Thanksgiving. Pinot Noir also works well since it complements most side dishes.

At homes across the country on Thanksgiving, the tables are filled with side dishes, too. A few Stew Leonard's creations you might like to try are Pears and Pecan Holiday Stuffing (page 125), Vermont Cheddar Mashed Potatoes (page 95), Savory Herb-Roasted Carrots (page 70), Holiday Favorite Green Beans Almondine (page 74), and Sage-Roasted Butternut Squash (page 90).

In our family, we like to cap off Thanksgiving dinner with a delicious dessert. Port Wine Cake (page 304) and French-Style Apple Tarte (page 288) are two of my family's favorites.

May you and your family have much to be thankful for this year, and always.

FISH AND SHELLFISH

Stew Leonard's receives fresh seafood shipments every day so our customers have a wide selection from which to choose. We sell so much fish that we have to replenish the supply in our fish cases every few hours.

One popular type of fish is swordfish, and Stew Leonard's sells about 3,000 pounds of it each week. In the summer, it's brought here right from fishing boats off Montauk, Long Island, and Cape May, New Jersey. In this book, you'll find several tasty swordfish recipes, including Grilled Swordfish Club (page 242).

Tuna is a great grilling and sautéing fish. We buy only sushi-grade tuna, which has superior freshness. When tuna goes on sale, it flies out of the store to the tune of 7,000 pounds a week. I think you'll enjoy our tuna recipes, especially Sesame-Crusted Yellowfin Tuna (page 250).

Customers at Stew Leonard's are buying more salmon than ever, both fresh and smoked. Stew Leonard's smokes our salmon in-store, and we sell about 1 ton of it each week. Check out our recipe for Poached Salmon in White Wine (page 251).

Shrimp, which is so easy to cook, is always a big seller, so here we offer you 10 Winning Ways to WOW Shrimp (page 226). We sell 50 tons of shrimp during the Christmas holidays alone!

In our stores, we carry big, sweet sea scallops as well as tiny bay scallops. We sell about 500 pounds of scallops each week. They're especially tasty as Seared Scallops with Tomato and Bacon (page 260).

We sell live lobsters from Maine and Canada. We keep our lobsters in specially designed tanks, just like the ones used by our lobstermen. You'll find several great lobster recipes in this book, as well as 10 Winning Ways to WOW Lobster (page 262).

10 Winning Ways to WOW

Shrimp

Shrimp is one of the most popular seafoods, possibly because it's so quick cooking.

1. SOUTHERN SPICED SHRIMP: Place a steamer basket in a pot with 1 inch of water. The basket should just touch the water, so adjust accordingly. Add 2 pounds medium shrimp (shells on) and sprinkle with ¼ cup Old Bay Seasoning. Cover and steam the fish for 5 minutes, or just until opaque. Remove to a plate and drizzle with a squeeze of lemon wedge. Makes 8 servings.

2. CREOLE SHRIMP: Heat 2 tablespoons olive oil in a large skillet over medium-high heat. Add 1 onion, chopped, and 1 rib celery, chopped. Cook, stirring frequently, for 4 minutes. Add 1 can (14.5 ounces) Creole-style diced tomatoes and ½ teaspoon thyme, crushed. Bring to a boil. Reduce the heat to low and stir in 1½ pounds medium peeled and deveined shrimp. Cook for 3 minutes, or just until opaque. Serve over hot cooked rice. Makes 6 servings.

3. SHRIMP TACOS: Toss 1 pound medium peeled and deveined shrimp with Southwest Rub mixture (page 213). Let stand for 5 minutes. Heat 1 tablespoon olive oil in a large skillet over medium-high heat. Add the shrimp and cook, stirring constantly, for 3 minutes, or just until opaque. Place on 1 side of a platter with shredded cheese, chopped tomatoes, shredded lettuce, and prepared salsa and guacamole. Serve with 8 prepared taco shells or burritos. Makes 4 to 6 servings.

4. SIMPLE SHRIMP SALAD: Bring a large pot of salted water to a boil. Fill a large bowl with ice water. Add 1 pound large shrimp to the boiling water. Cook for 3 minutes, or until just opaque. Drain and plunge into the ice water. Peel and devein the shrimp, removing the tail also. Place in a bowl and toss with ½ cup Lemon-Chive Dressing (page 50). Arrange 1 cup mesclun on 4 each of salad plates. Evenly divide the shrimp among the plates. Makes 4 servings.

5. SHRIMP IN LIGHT CURRY SAUCE: Peel, devein, and rinse 1½ pounds medium shrimp. Heat 1 tablespoon olive oil in a large nonstick pan over medium-high heat. Add ½ cup finely chopped onion, ¼ pound finely chopped celery, ½ cup peeled and diced apple, and 1 teaspoon minced garlic. Season with salt and freshly ground black pepper to taste. Cook over medium heat until the ingredients have wilted. Do not brown. Add the shrimp, 1 bay leaf, and 1 tablespoon curry powder. Cook, stirring often, for about 3 minutes over high heat. Add 1 tablespoon lemon juice, ½ cup sour cream, and 1 cup plain yogurt. Stir. Gently bring the mixture to a boil while stirring. Check seasonings. Remove the bay leaf. Sprinkle with 2 teaspoons chopped cilantro and serve immediately. Makes 4 servings.

6. GINGER-LIME SHRIMP: Preheat the grill to medium-high. In a large bowl, whisk together the juice of 2 limes, ½ cup teriyaki sauce, ⅓ cup honey, 2 tablespoons grated fresh gingerroot, and 1 chopped Chinese, Thai, or habanero chile. Add 1 pound jumbo shrimp, peeled with shelled tail on and butterflied. Toss to coat well. Cover and refrigerate for 20 minutes to 1 hour. Using a slotted spoon, remove the shrimp from the marinade, discarding the marinade. Place the shrimp in a grill pan or directly on the grill rack and cook for 3 minutes, or until curled and opaque, turning once. Garnish with fresh lime slices. Makes 2 to 4 servings.

7. SHRIMP AND BROCCOLI STIR-FRY: Heat 1 tablespoon vegetable oil in a large skillet over medium-high heat. Add 1 pound large peeled and deveined shrimp, and cook for 3 minutes, or just until pink.

Remove to a bowl. Increase the heat to high and add 1 clove garlic, minced; 3 cups broccoli florets; 2 cups shiitake mushrooms; 1 tablespoon grated gingerroot; and ½ cup water. Bring to a boil and cook, stirring, for 3 minutes. In a small cup, combine 3 tablespoons soy sauce, 3 tablespoons wine vinegar, 2 teaspoons cornstarch, and 2 teaspoons sesame oil. Add to the skillet and cook for 3 minutes, or until thickened. Add the shrimp to the skillet and cook 1 minute. Makes 4 servings.

8. SHRIMP IN CREAM SAUCE: In a small saucepan over medium heat, bring ½ cup dry white wine; 1 tablespoon white wine vinegar; 1 shallot, minced; 1 tablespoon fresh chopped tarragon; and ½ teaspoon salt to a boil. Boil for 10 minutes, or until reduced by half. Reduce the heat to low and whisk in 4 tablespoons butter and 2 tablespoons heavy cream. Meanwhile, melt 1 tablespoon butter over medium heat. Add 1 pound medium peeled and deveined shrimp and cook, stirring, for 3

minutes, or just until opaque. Stir into the sauce and serve over cooked angel hair pasta or rice. Makes 4 servings.

9. BALSAMIC-GLAZED SHRIMP: In a small saucepan over high heat, bring 2 cups balsamic vinegar to a boil. Reduce the heat to medium-high and cook for about 40 minutes, or until the vinegar is reduced to about ¾ cup. Melt 1 tablespoon butter over medium heat. Add 1 pound medium peeled and deveined shrimp and cook, stirring, for 3 minutes, or just until opaque. Serve drizzled with the balsamic glaze. Makes 4 servings.

10. GRILLED SHRIMP WITH HORSE-RADISH SAUCE: In a small bowl, whisk together ¾ cup sour cream; ¼ cup mayonnaise; 2 tablespoons prepared horseradish; 2 scallions, minced; and a dash of hot sauce. Season 2 pounds large peeled and deveined shrimp with salt and pepper. Grill or broil for 4 minutes, or until just opaque. Serve with the horseradish sauce. Makes 8 servings.

STEW'S FAVORITE ZUPPA DI PESCE

1 pound linguine

2 tablespoons extra-virgin olive oil

2 cloves garlic, minced

1 jar (26 ounces) prepared marinara sauce

1 bottle (8 ounces) clam juice

½ cup white wine, such as Chardonnay or Pinot Grigio

1 pound large shrimp, peeled and deveined

2 lobster tails, thawed if frozen

1 pound tuna, halibut, or scrod, cut into 1-inch pieces

WINE PAIRING

Chianti Classico
or
Super Tuscans

30 MINUTES OR LESS

Prepare the linguine according to the package directions.

Meanwhile, heat the oil in a large skillet over medium-high heat. Add the garlic and cook for 4 minutes, or until golden brown. Add the marinara sauce, clam juice, and wine. Bring to a boil. Reduce the heat to medium and simmer. Add the shrimp, lobster, and fish and cook for 6 minutes, or until the fish is just opaque. Drain the pasta and place in a large shallow serving bowl. Top with the zuppa di pesce. *Makes 6 to 8 servings.*

COOKING TIP

Feel free to substitute mussels, clams, swordfish, or scallops for the seafood mentioned.

COCONUT SHRIMP WITH PINEAPPLE SALSA

1 cup fresh pineapple, finely chopped

¼ cup red onion, diced

¼ cup red bell pepper, diced

2 tablespoons fresh cilantro, chopped

1 clove garlic, minced

1 can coconut milk

1 pound (16 to 20) shrimp, deveined, peeled, and butterflied

Canola oil

¼ cup plain bread crumbs

1 cup shredded sweetened coconut

1 teaspoon salt

½ teaspoon black pepper

2 large eggs, beaten

WINE PAIRING

Sauvignon Blanc

30 MINUTES OR LESS

STORING TIP

To store fresh shrimp, place a colander filled with ice in a large bowl. Top with the shrimp. Cover loosely with plastic wrap and store in the refrigerator for up to 1 day.

In a bowl, toss together the pineapple, onion, bell pepper, cilantro, and garlic. Set aside.

In another bowl, place the coconut milk. Add the shrimp and toss to coat.

In a large skillet or fryer, heat 4 inches of oil to 350°F.

In a third bowl, combine the bread crumbs, coconut, salt, and black pepper. Mix well.

In a fourth bowl, place the eggs.

Remove the shrimp from the coconut milk and place in the bowl with the eggs. Place the shrimp in the bread crumb mixture, pressing to coat well. Fry the shrimp for 3 to 4 minutes, or until golden brown and opaque. Serve the shrimp with the pineapple salsa. ***Makes 4 servings.***

COOKING TIP

The term "butterflied" means to cut down the center so that it lays flat. Place the shrimp on a cutting board and make a slice ¾ of the way through the middle of it to lay it open flat. Then pound the shrimp with a heavy pan or mallet so it is the same thickness all over.

This risotto is easy and quick to prepare.

CROWD-PLEASING SHRIMP RISOTTO

4 cups chicken broth

3 tablespoons butter

8 large shrimp, peeled, deveined, and chopped

3 shallots, minced

2 cloves garlic, minced

1½ cups long grain or Arborio rice

½ cup white wine

½ cup grated Parmesan cheese

2 tablespoons chopped fresh sage leaves

Sage leaves for garnish

WINE PAIRING

Pinot Grigio

30 MINUTES OR LESS

In a medium saucepan, bring the broth to a boil over high heat. Reduce the temperature to low and simmer.

In a large saucepan, melt the butter over medium-high heat. Add the shrimp, shallots, and garlic and cook for 2 minutes, or until tender. Add the rice and cook, stirring often, for about 5 minutes, or until the rice becomes opaque. Add the wine and cook until evaporated. Stir the hot broth, 1 cup at a time, into the rice. Cook, stirring constantly, for about 3 minutes, or until the rice absorbs the broth. Repeat until all of the broth has been absorbed and the rice is tender and creamy with a slightly firm bite, about 15 minutes. Stir in the cheese and chopped sage and cook, stirring constantly for 2 minutes. Garnish with sage leaves. ***Makes 6 servings.***

SHRIMP WITH CREAMY GARLIC SAUCE OVER LINGUINE

1 pound linguine

4 tablespoons butter, divided

1 pound medium shrimp, peeled and deveined

1 medium onion, diced

¼ cup all-purpose flour

2 cloves garlic, minced

½ teaspoon white pepper

2 cups chicken broth

½ cup white wine

2 cups heavy cream

1 tablespoon chopped parsley

WINE PAIRING

Tocai Friulano

30 MINUTES OR LESS

STORING TIP

Frozen shrimp may be stored in the freezer in airtight zip-top freezer bags for up to 2 months.

Prepare the linguine according to the package directions.

Meanwhile, melt 2 tablespoons of the butter in a large skillet over medium-high heat. Working in batches, add the shrimp and cook, stirring frequently for 3 minutes, or until pink and cooked through. With a slotted spoon, remove the shrimp to a bowl and keep warm.

Melt the remaining 2 tablespoons butter in the skillet. Add the onion and cook for 5 minutes, or until softened. Stir in the flour, garlic, and pepper and cook for 5 minutes, stirring constantly. Add the broth, wine, and cream and bring to a boil. Cook 4 minutes, or until thickened. Stir in the parsley and remove from the heat. Stir in the shrimp.

Drain the linguine and place in a large serving bowl. Top with the sauce, tossing to coat well. *Makes 8 servings.*

SHOPPING TIP

Shrimp, a crustacean, is America's favorite shellfish. Most of the shrimp we consume comes from the Atlantic coast, Pacific coast, or Gulf coast. Almost all shrimp is frozen at sea, so at fish counters, frozen ones are just as good as thawed.

FISH FILLET WITH CITRUS BEURRE BLANC SAUCE

1 orange

4 skinless fish fillets, such as sole, scrod, halibut, or tilapia (about 1¾ pounds)

½ teaspoon salt

6 tablespoons cold butter, divided

½ cup white wine

1 shallot, minced

1 tablespoon lime juice

Pinot Grigio or Sauvignon Blanc

From the orange, grate 1 teaspoon zest and squeeze ¼ cup juice. Set aside. Sprinkle the fish with the salt.

Melt 1 tablespoon of the butter in a large nonstick skillet over medium heat. Add the fish and cook, turning once, for about 3 minutes, or until golden brown. Add the wine, shallot, orange juice, and orange zest and bring just to a simmer. Simmer for 3 to 7 minutes, or until the fish is opaque and just cooked through. With a slotted spatula, remove the fish from the skillet to a serving dish. Keep warm.

Increase the heat to high and boil the liquid until thickened and reduced to about ¼ cup. Cut the remaining butter into pieces. Remove the skillet from the heat and whisk in the butter until melted and creamy. Whisk in the lime juice. Pour the sauce over the fish. ***Makes 4 servings.***

Fresh fish fillets are bathed in an orange butter sauce spiked with lime juice. Serve this with Holiday Favorite Green Beans Almondine (page 74).

COOKING TIP

Beurre blanc literally means "white butter" but refers to a sauce made with white wine, shallots, and vinegar or citrus juice. The sauce is reduced then thickened by whisking in cold butter.

CUSTOMER RECIPE COOK-OFF

Edward has been an art teacher at Norwalk High School for 30 years. He is very happily married, with two sons and two stepsons.

"I have been shopping at Stew Leonard's since I started working in Norwalk in 1973. Having taught in Norwalk for so many years, I have several former students working at Stew Leonard's, so many shopping trips turn into mini reunions," says Edward.

Edward's inspiration for the recipe came from a restaurant in Trumbull, Connecticut, that serves swordfish stuffed with eggplant and mozzarella. Edward enjoyed the dish and tried making it himself. Edward recalls, "I didn't have much success with the eggplant-mozzarella stuffing, so I experimented with other ingredients. The arugula-Gorgonzola mixture is my favorite. It is really quite simple and easy. The only special need is a good sharp knife to cut the pocket."

EDWARD WARNER'S
ARUGULA-STUFFED GRILLED SWORDFISH

4 tablespoons olive oil, divided

2 large cloves garlic, thinly sliced

1½ cups arugula leaves, coarsely chopped

¼ cup crumbled Gorgonzola cheese

¼ teaspoon salt, divided

¼ teaspoon ground black pepper, divided

2 swordfish steaks, 1 inch thick (about 8 to 12 ounces each)

Preheat the grill. Soak 8 thick toothpicks in water.

Heat 3 tablespoons of the oil in a large skillet over medium-high heat. Add the garlic and cook for 2 minutes, stirring, until lightly browned. Remove from the heat and stir in the arugula, cheese, ⅛ teaspoon of the salt, and ⅛ teaspoon of the pepper. Set aside.

Place the swordfish steaks on a cutting board. With a sharp paring knife, working parallel to the board, cut a 3-inch pocket into each steak. Cut through the meat to 1 inch from the sides. Stuff the arugula mixture into the pocket, securing the edges with the toothpicks. Coat the steaks with the remaining 1 tablespoon oil and season with the remaining salt and pepper. Grill over medium heat, turning once, for 4 minutes, or until the swordfish flakes easily when tested with a fork. *Makes 2 servings.*

SWORDFISH VERA CRUZ

4 swordfish steaks

2 tablespoons lime juice

½ teaspoon salt

2 tablespoons olive oil

1 small onion, chopped

1 small green bell pepper, chopped

2 cloves garlic, minced

2 cups fresh prepared salsa

¼ cup pimiento-stuffed olives, coarsely chopped

1 tablespoon capers

WINE PAIRING

Pinot Noir or Sauvignon Blanc

30 MINUTES OR LESS

Place the swordfish on a large plate and sprinkle with the lime juice and salt. Set aside.

Heat the oil in a large skillet over medium-high heat. Add the onion and pepper and cook for 5 minutes, or until tender. Add the garlic and cook for 1 minute, stirring constantly. Add the salsa, olives, and capers and bring to a boil. Reduce the heat to low and place the swordfish on the sauce. Cover and simmer for 8 to 10 minutes, or until the swordfish flakes easily when tested with a fork. ***Makes 4 servings.***

Olives and capers turn prepared salsa into a pungent sauce—a perfect balance to sweet swordfish.

COOKING TIP

Dishes labeled Vera Cruz are fashioned after a classic from the Mexican city of the same name. Typically, fish is topped with a mixture of peppers, onions, tomatoes, olives, and capers. Any fish will work here, but favorites for this dish include snapper, bass, or orange roughy.

GRILLED SWORDFISH CLUB

4 pieces skinless swordfish steaks, each ½-inch thick (about 1½ pounds)

¼ cup olive oil

3 tablespoons lemon juice, divided

2 tablespoons fresh chopped tarragon, divided

½ teaspoon salt

1 teaspoon black pepper, divided

¼ cup mayonnaise

2 tablespoons sour cream

6 leaves romaine lettuce

1 large tomato, chopped

4 slices crisp cooked bacon

1 lemon, cut into wedges

WINE PAIRING

Pinot Grigio

GREAT ON THE GRILL

Lay each swordfish piece on a cutting board and cut horizontally in half.

In a pie plate or baking dish, whisk together the oil, 2 tablespoons of the lemon juice, 1 tablespoon of the tarragon, the salt, and ½ teaspoon of the pepper. Add the fish to the marinade and set aside for 20 minutes.

Meanwhile, in a small bowl, combine the mayonnaise, sour cream, the remaining l tablespoon lemon juice, the remaining 1 tablespoon tarragon, and the remaining ½ teaspoon pepper.

In another bowl, combine the lettuce, tomato, and bacon.

Preheat the grill. Grill each side of the swordfish for about 5 minutes.

Combine the salad with the dressing, tossing to coat well. Place 1 piece of swordfish on 4 dinner plates. Evenly divide the salad mixture among the fish. Top each with the remaining 4 pieces of swordfish. Insert a toothpick into 2 sides of the "club" and cut diagonally. Serve with the lemon. **Makes 4 servings.**

BAKED COD BELLA VISTA

4 skinless codfish fillets (about 1½ pounds)

½ teaspoon salt

2 tablespoons butter

2 shallots, chopped

¼ cup white wine

1 medium green bell pepper, sliced into 8 rings

1 medium onion, cut into 8 slices

2 medium tomatoes, cut into 8 slices

WINE PAIRING

Chardonnay

30 MINUTES OR LESS

Preheat the oven to 375°F. Sprinkle the fish with the salt.

In a large oven-proof skillet, melt the butter over medium-high heat. Add the shallots and cook for 3 minutes. Add the wine and the fish. Top each fillet with 2 slices of bell pepper, onion, and tomato. Cover the skillet with a lid or aluminum foil. Bake for 5 minutes. Remove the cover, baste the fish with the sauce, and cook for 3 minutes, or until the fish is opaque and flakes easily when tested with a fork. ***Makes 4 servings.***

SHOPPING TIP

Be sure to buy fish from a quality seller. The fish should be stored on ice and very cold. It should smell fresh and not "fishy." The skin of whole fish should be clean, shiny, and firm. Fillets should have bright, vibrant colors. Browning around the edges of fillets shows aging.

FAST FISH KEBABS

1 pound skinless firm fish, such as halibut, salmon, shark, swordfish, or tuna, cut into 24 pieces (about 1½ inches each)

24 cherry tomatoes

12 large scallions, white and light green part only, each cut in half to form 1½-inch pieces

½ cup Simple Herb Vinaigrette (page 51)

Sauvignon Blanc

GREAT ON THE GRILL

If using wooden skewers, soak in water for 30 minutes.

Preheat the grill.

Using 8 skewers, thread the fish, tomatoes, and scallions. Brush with about half of the vinaigrette. Grill, turning occasionally, for 7 to 10 minutes, or until the fish is opaque. Brush with the remaining vinaigrette and serve. **Makes 4 servings.**

COOKING TIP

If you don't have time to prepare the vinaigrette, a bottled Italian or balsamic dressing will work well.

This is great served over rice.

FILET DE SOLE MARGUERY

3 shallots, minced

8 sole fillets

8 caps mushrooms, cooked

8 shrimp, peeled and deveined

8 large oysters

½ cup dry white wine

½ cup clam juice

1 tablespoon lemon juice

½ teaspoon salt

¼ teaspoon black pepper

2 large egg yolks

½ cup light cream

2 tablespoons butter

2 tablespoons all-purpose flour

1 cup whole milk

8 thin slices truffle (optional)

WINE PAIRING

Pinot Grigio

Preheat the oven to 475°F.

Grease a 13- × 9-inch baking dish and add the shallots. Arrange the sole over the shallots. On each piece of sole, place 1 mushroom, 1 shrimp, and 1 oyster. Add the wine, clam juice, lemon juice, salt, and pepper. Cover with foil and bake for 8 minutes, or until the sole is opaque. Remove the sole and place on an oven-safe plate. Cover loosely with foil. Increase the oven temperature to broil.

Meanwhile, whisk together the egg yolks and cream. Set aside.

In a small skillet, melt the butter over medium-high heat. Add the flour and cook for 2 minutes, stirring constantly. Gradually whisk in the milk. Cook for 5 minutes, stirring constantly, or until thickened. Remove about 1 cup of the sauce and whisk into the bowl with the egg yolks. Gradually whisk the egg yolk mixture back into the saucepan. Bring to a boil. Remove from the heat.

Strain the cooking liquid from the fish into a small saucepan. Discard the shallots. Bring the liquid to a boil and boil for 7 minutes or until reduced by half. Whisk into the cream sauce

Pour the sauce over the sole. Place the platter in the preheated broiler or under a salamander until golden brown. Garnish with a thick slice of truffle on each fillet, if desired. ***Makes 8 servings.***

STORING TIP

Wrap fish in plastic wrap and store it in the refrigerator for up to 2 days.

GRILLED TUNA WITH PESTO AND WALNUTS

¼ cup walnuts

1 clove garlic

½ cup olive oil

1½ cups loosely packed basil leaves

¼ cup Romano cheese

¼ cup lemon juice

4 tuna steaks (about 1½ pounds)

½ teaspoon salt

¼ teaspoon black pepper

WINE PAIRING

Merlot or Chardonnay

30 MINUTES OR LESS

STORING TIP

Fish freezes well but should be frozen only once. Be sure to ask at the seafood department if what you are buying is fresh or previously frozen. If it's been frozen already, buy it only if you will cook it that day. When you freeze fresh fish, do it as soon as you get home. Place it in a zip-top freezer bag, date it, and seal it well. Use it within 3 months.

To thaw frozen fish quickly, keep it sealed tightly in the bag and place it in a bowl of cool water.

Oil the grill rack and preheat the grill.

In a food processor or blender, process the walnuts, garlic, and ¼ cup of the oil until fine. Add the basil. On top of the basil put the cheese, lemon juice, and 3 tablespoons of the oil. Puree until smooth and bright green. Add more oil if necessary.

Brush the tuna with 1 tablespoon of the oil. Sprinkle with the salt and pepper. Grill the tuna for 6 to 8 minutes or until cooked through. Place on a serving plate and drizzle with the pesto sauce. ***Makes 4 servings.***

COOKING TIP

When cooking fish, think of the general rule that fish should be cooked for 10 minutes per inch of thickness. Typically, fish should be cooked until it flakes easily when tested with a fork. If you use a thermometer, it should reach 145°F. Today, many folks prefer some fish, such as tuna, cooked on the rare side. This would call for shorter cooking times. When cooking to rare, opt for sushi-grade tuna, the finest and safest grade available.

SESAME-CRUSTED YELLOWFIN TUNA

2 large egg whites

2 tablespoons black sesame seeds

2 tablespoons white sesame seeds

4 yellowfin tuna steaks (8 ounces each)

2 tablespoons canola or vegetable oil

¼ cup soy sauce

1 teaspoon minced fresh ginger

WINE PAIRING

Pinot Noir

Preheat the oven to 400°F.

In a bowl, whisk the egg whites until frothy.

In a shallow bowl, combine the black and white sesame seeds. Dip the tuna into the egg whites and then dredge in the sesame seeds to form an even crust.

GREAT ON THE GRILL

In a large skillet, heat the oil over medium-high heat. Add the tuna and cook for 6 minutes, turning once, or until the tuna is golden brown.

Meanwhile, in a saucepan, cook the soy sauce and ginger over medium heat for 3 minutes, or until warmed.

Serve the tuna with the sauce. ***Makes 4 servings.***

SHOPPING TIP

When buying, plan on ½ pound of boneless fillet per person, ¾ pound of cleaned fish on the bone per person, and 1 pound of whole fish per person.

POACHED SALMON IN WHITE WINE

½ cup white wine

1 small onion, sliced

½ teaspoon salt

½ teaspoon peppercorn mixture

4 salmon fillets (5 to 6 ounces each)

1 tablespoon butter

1 teaspoon capers

WINE PAIRING

Chardonnay

30 MINUTES OR LESS

In a large skillet, combine the wine, ½ cup water, onion, salt, and peppercorns. Bring to a boil over high heat. Reduce the heat to low and bring to a simmer.

Add the salmon fillets skin-sides down. If the liquid does not cover the salmon, spoon some of the liquid over it. Cover and simmer for 8 minutes, or just until the salmon flakes. Remove the salmon to a plate and keep warm.

Bring the liquid to a boil. Cook for 10 minutes, or until reduced to about ¼ cup. Whisk in the butter and the capers.

Remove the skin from the salmon and top with the sauce. ***Makes 4 servings.***

SHOPPING TIP

> Most customers prefer filleted salmon because they don't have to worry about bones.

BLACKENED SALMON WITH MANGO SALSA

¼ cup mango puree

2 tablespoons lemon juice

½ teaspoon cumin

1 mango, halved, seeded, removed from the skin, and diced

¼ cup minced red pepper

¼ cup minced red onion

¼ cup minced cilantro

1 tablespoon Cajun spice

1 tablespoon paprika

1 teaspoon salt

4 skinless salmon fillets (about 1½ pounds)

2 tablespoons olive oil

4 cups mesclun or gourmet lettuce

Riesling or Viognier

In a serving bowl, whisk together the mango puree, lemon juice, and cumin. Add the mango, pepper, onion, and cilantro. Toss to coat well. Set aside.

In a small bowl, combine the Cajun spice, paprika, and salt. Place the salmon on a cutting board and spread the spice mixture over the salmon.

In a large skillet, heat the oil over medium-high heat. Add the salmon and cook for 6 minutes, turning once, or until the salmon is just opaque in the center.

Place 1 cup of the mesclun onto 4 dinner plates. Top each with a salmon fillet. Evenly divide the mango salsa over the salmon. ***Makes 4 servings.***

COOKING TIP

Mangoes are pear-shaped tropical fruits with a sweet, tender flesh and a green skin with a red blush.

Mangoes contain a large, flat seed in the center. The best way to remove this seed and release the fruit is to hold the fruit upright and cut down the center of each side of the pit.

Working with one half at a time, score the flesh into cubes, being sure not to cut through the skin. Hold one half with two hands and press the skin upward, turning the flesh inside out.

Slice off the cubes or eat them right from the skin.

ROASTED SALMON WITH VINE-RIPENED TOMATOES

Olive oil

1 pound salmon fillet, trimmed, bones removed, and cut into 4 pieces

½ teaspoon salt

½ teaspoon cracked black pepper

½ teaspoon dried oregano

1 tablespoon finely shredded fresh basil leaves

2 large plum tomatoes, sliced

Salt

WINE PAIRING

Pinot Noir or Sauvignon Blanc

30 MINUTES OR LESS

Preheat the oven to 350°F.

Lightly oil a baking sheet. Place the salmon on the sheet and coat the salmon with the salt, pepper, oregano, and basil. Top each piece of salmon with slices of tomato to cover. Season the salmon with additional salt to taste.

Bake for 6 to 8 minutes, or until just opaque in the center. ***Makes 4 servings.***

SHOPPING TIP

Don't buy fish on price alone. Previously frozen fish that is thawed is less expensive than fresh, but the quality is not the same.

SALMON STEAKS WITH PINEAPPLE SALSA

1½ cups diced fresh pineapple or drained canned unsweetened chunks

¼ cup minced red bell pepper

¼ cup minced green bell pepper

¼ cup minced red onion

¼ cup chopped fresh cilantro

1 tablespoon fresh lime juice

1½ teaspoons minced seeded jalapeño chiles

¼ teaspoon grated lime peel

¼ teaspoon salt

4 salmon steaks, ¾-inch thick (6 to 8 ounces each)

1 tablespoon low-sodium soy sauce

WINE PAIRING

Chardonnay

30 MINUTES OR LESS

In a serving bowl, combine the pineapple, red pepper, green pepper, onion, cilantro, lime juice, jalapeño, lime peel, and salt. Toss to coat well. Cover and refrigerate. (This can be prepared 6 hours ahead.)

Preheat the broiler. Brush the salmon steaks with the soy sauce and place on a rack in a broiler pan. Broil for 6 minutes, turning once, or until just opaque in center. Serve the salmon with the salsa. ***Makes 4 servings.***

HORSERADISH-CRUSTED SALMON WITH SHRIMP SAUCE

1 cup panko bread crumbs

¼ cup butter, melted

1 tablespoon prepared horseradish

1 teaspoon lemon juice

1 teaspoon paprika

½ teaspoon dried dill

1 teaspoon salt

¼ teaspoon white pepper

2 skinless salmon fillets (8 ounces each)

2 teaspoon olive oil, divided

4 large shrimp (shell on)

½ cup white wine

1 cup heavy cream

WINE PAIRING

Riesling or Albariño

30 MINUTES OR LESS

SHOPPING TIP

Panko bread crumbs are used in Japanese cooking for coating fried foods. They are coarser than those usually used in the United States.

Preheat the oven to 400°F.

In a small mixing bowl, combine the bread crumbs, butter, horseradish, lemon juice, paprika, dill, salt, and pepper. Blend well by hand. Set aside at room temperature.

Brush the salmon with 1 teaspoon of the oil and place on small metal baking sheet pan. Top each salmon fillet with an even amount of the bread crumb mixture, pressing down lightly.

Bake the salmon for about 20 minutes, or until just opaque in the center.

Meanwhile, peel and devein the shrimp. Reserve the shells and dice the meat.

In a saucepan, heat the remaining 1 teaspoon oil over medium-high heat. Add the shrimp shells, stirring for 1 minute. Add the wine and bring to a boil. Add the cream and shrimp meat. Bring to a simmer and cook for 6 minutes, or until thickened. Strain the sauce, discarding the shells and meat.

Serve the salmon with the shrimp sauce. ***Makes 4 servings.***

COOKING TIP

It's fastest to prepare shrimp when you buy it peeled and deveined, but follow these easy steps if you have to devein it yourself.

With kitchen shears, cut into the outer curve, just deep enough into the flesh to expose the vein.

Rinse away the vein under cold running water while removing the shells.

SPICY GRILLED SALMON AND EGGPLANT

1 large eggplant

4 salmon steaks (about ½ pound each)

1 lime

1 lemon

¼ cup olive oil

1 teaspoon Greek or Italian seasoning

⅛ teaspoon hot red pepper flakes

¼ teaspoon freshly ground black pepper

2 cups hot cooked rice

WINE PAIRING

Pinot Noir or Zinfandel

GREAT ON THE GRILL

Remove the stem and end of the eggplant and slice on a diagonal, cutting slices approximately ¼ inch thick.

Place the eggplant slices and the salmon steaks in a glass 13- × 9-inch baking dish.

COOKING TIP

Salting eggplants before cooking is considered mandatory by some chefs who believe it reduces bitterness; others consider it unnecessary. It is time consuming, but if you prefer this method, peel and slice or chop the eggplant. Place it in a colander, sprinkle it with salt, and let it drain for 1 hour.

Cut the lemon and lime in half and squeeze the juice into a small bowl. Stir in the oil, seasoning, pepper flakes, and black pepper. Pour the mixture over the salmon steaks and eggplant. Cover and refrigerator for 1 to 1½ hours, turning the salmon and eggplants once.

Preheat the grill.

Place the salmon steaks on the grill and cook for 6 minutes, turning once, or until the salmon is just opaque in the center. After 2 minutes, add the eggplant to the grill and grill for 5 minutes, turning once, or until the eggplant is browned and tender. Serve the salmon steaks and eggplant with the rice. ***Makes 4 servings.***

SHOPPING TIP

The high oil content in salmon makes it a terrific fish to freeze. It will last for 3 months in your freezer. To defrost, put it in your refrigerator overnight.

SEARED SCALLOPS WITH TOMATO AND BACON

2 strips bacon, cut into ½-inch pieces

1 pound sea scallops, tough muscle removed

¼ teaspoon salt

¼ teaspoon ground black pepper

1 cup cherry tomatoes, halved

1 tablespoon chopped fresh basil or ½ teaspoon dried

¼ cup white wine

WINE PAIRING

Sauvignon Blanc

30 MINUTES OR LESS

In a large skillet over medium-high heat, cook the bacon for 5 minutes, or until browned. Using a slotted spoon, remove the bacon to a dish. Remove all but 2 tablespoons of the bacon drippings.

Meanwhile, season the scallops with the salt and pepper. Add the scallops to the skillet and cook, turning once, for 4 minutes, or until

SHOPPING TIP

Scallops' color varies. If you see all-white ones, they have probably been soaked in water, which increases their weight while reducing their flavor. Go for dry scallops, which haven't been soaked in water.

browned and just opaque in the center. Remove the scallops to the plate with the bacon. Add the tomatoes and basil to the skillet and cook, stirring constantly, for 3 minutes, or until tender. Stir in the wine and cook, stirring to break up the browned bits, for 2 minutes. Return the bacon, scallops, and any drippings to the skillet and heat for 1 minute. ***Makes 4 servings.***

COOKING TIP

Cook scallops the day you purchase them. Refrigerate them until you're ready to cook them.

Cook scallops for 3 to 4 minutes, or until they're opaque. Over- or undercooking makes scallops rubbery.

10 Winning Ways to WOW

Lobster

A favorite in restaurants, lobster is intimidating for some home cooks. Fear not—these simple recipes will make lobster a family favorite. Be sure to see the many tips on page 269 for all you'll need to know about preparing lobster.

1. BOILED LOBSTERS: Fill a large pot with salted water. Cover and bring to a boil over high heat. Add the lobsters headfirst. Begin timing and cook accordingly: 8 minutes for a 1-pound lobster, 15 minutes for a 2-pound lobster, or 22 minutes for a 3-pound lobster. Using tongs, remove the lobsters to the sink. If eating warm, drain the liquid and serve. If eating cold, place into ice water for 30 minutes to cool. Refrigerate until ready to use.

2. STEAMED LOBSTERS: Place 2 inches of salted water in a large pot. Place a steamer rack in the pot. Cover and bring to a boil. Place the lobsters on the rack, cover, and cook accordingly: 10 minutes for a 1-pound lobster, 18 minutes for a 2-pound lobster, or 25 minutes for a 3-pound lobster. Using tongs, remove the lobsters to the sink. If eating warm, drain the liquid and serve. If eating cold, place into ice water for 30 minutes to cool. Refrigerate until ready to use.

3. STUFFED AND BAKED LOBSTERS: Preheat the oven to 425°F. Split the lobster down the middle of the underside but not all the way through. Remove and discard the head sac and intestine. Crack the claws. Loosely add the stuffing of your choice (seasoned bread crumbs, for example), into the split tail. Brush the tail and stuffing with melted butter. Bake accordingly: 15 minutes for a 1-pound lobster, 24 minutes for a 2-pound lobster, or 28 minutes for a 3-pound lobster. Using tongs, remove to a serving plate.

4. GRILLED LOBSTER TAILS: Preheat the grill. Cut 2 frozen lobster tails, thawed (about 10 to 12 ounces each), in half lengthwise. Brush the tails with 2 tablespoons olive oil. Place, meat sides down, on the grill. Grill for 4 minutes. Turn over and grill for 4 minutes longer, or until opaque in the center. Makes 2 servings.

5. TOMATO AND LOBSTER PASTA SALAD: Prepare 1 pound shell pasta according to the package directions. Meanwhile, seed 2 pounds beefsteak tomatoes and chop into 1-inch pieces. Heat ¼ cup extra-virgin olive oil in a large skillet over medium-high heat. Add 1 shallot, minced, and cook for 2 minutes. Add the tomatoes and cook for 2 minutes longer. Remove from the heat and stir in 1 pound cooked lobster meat, cut into bite-size pieces, and 2 tablespoons chopped fresh basil,

cilantro, or dill. Add the drained pasta and toss to coat. Makes 4 to 6 servings.

6. ROASTED VEGETABLES WITH LOBSTER: Preheat the oven to 425°F. In a large roasting pan, combine 1 large red onion, chopped; 2 bell peppers, chopped; 8 ounces mushrooms, quartered; 3 tablespoons olive oil; ½ teaspoon salt; and ¼ teaspoon ground black pepper. Toss to coat well. Roast the vegetables, turning once, for 40 minutes, or until browned. Meanwhile, in a large serving bowl, whisk together 1 tablespoon olive oil and 1 tablespoon white wine vinegar. Add 2 bunches arugula, the roasted vegetables, and 1 pound cooked lobster meat, cut into bite-size pieces. Toss to coat well. Makes 4 to 6 servings.

7. CHEF CHAZ'S LOBSTER AND BOW-TIE PASTA SALAD: In a small saucepan, heat 1 teaspoon canola oil over medium-high heat. Add 1 minced shallot and 1 teaspoon cracked black pepper and cook for 3 minutes, or until softened. Add 1 tablespoon dried tarragon and 2 tablespoons white wine vinegar. Reduce the heat to low and simmer for 3 minutes, or until the liquid has evaporated. Pour into a large bowl to cool. When the mixture has cooled, stir in ¾ cup mayonnaise. Meanwhile, prepare 1 pound bow-tie pasta according to the package directions. Add 1 cup frozen tender tiny peas to the pasta water during the last 2 minutes of cooking. Drain the pasta and peas. Run under cold water and drain completely. Add the drained pasta, peas, and 1 pound cooked lobster meat to the bowl. Toss to coat well. Arrange 1 head Belgian endive, separated, in a circle around the edges of a large serving platter. Place the salad in the center of the leaves. Makes 8 to 12 servings.

8. LOBSTER SALAD IN AVOCADO BOATS: Prepare Cheesy Chopped Avocado Salad (page 60), reserving the 4 avocado-shell halves. Add 1 pound cooked lobster meat, cut into bite-size pieces, to the salad. Place 1 shell on each of 4 lunch plates and fill with the salad. Serve with bread sticks. Makes 4 servings.

9. LOBSTER ROLLS: In a small bowl, toss together 1 pound cooked lobster meat, cut into bite-size pieces, and ⅓ cup Lemon-Chive Dressing (page 50). Arrange 4 hot dog rolls on a serving plate. Fill with lettuce leaves, tomato slices, and the lobster salad. Makes 4 servings.

10. LOBSTER AND MUSHROOM SAUTÉ: Heat 2 tablespoons olive oil and 2 tablespoons butter in a large skillet over medium-high heat. Add 1 pound assorted mushrooms, sliced. Cook for 10 minutes, or until the mushrooms begin to brown. Add 1 clove garlic, minced, and 2 teaspoons chopped fresh tarragon and cook for 1 minute. Stir in ¼ cup white wine and cook until almost evaporated. Stir in ½ cup heavy cream and cook for 2 minutes, or until thickened. Stir in 1 pound cooked lobster meat, cut into bite-size pieces. Toast 4 large slices semolina, Italian, or French bread. Place on 4 plates and top each with ¼ of the lobster mixture. Makes 4 servings.

LOBSTER THERMIDOR WITH SALSA BALSAMELLA

2 cooked whole lobsters, cut lengthwise in half (about 1½ pounds)

1 tablespoon olive oil

4 scallions, minced

1 small green bell pepper, minced

4 ounces mushrooms, minced

2 tablespoons chopped fresh tarragon or 1 tablespoon dried tarragon

¼ teaspoon black pepper

¼ cup brandy

¼ cup white wine

½ cup clam juice

3 tablespoons butter

3 tablespoons all-purpose flour

1½ cups whole milk

1 teaspoon Dijon mustard

⅓ cup fresh grated Parmesan cheese

WINE PAIRING

Chardonnay or white Burgundy

Keep the lobster shells intact and carefully remove the meat from the bodies. Place the shells on 4 dinner plates. Chop the meat and tomalley and place in a bowl. Set aside.

In a medium skillet, heat the oil over medium-high heat. Add the scallions, bell pepper, mushrooms, tarragon, and black pepper. Cook for 2 to 3 minutes, until softened. Add the brandy and wine and turn the heat to high.

When the liquid is boiling, add the clam juice. Reduce the heat to medium and cook for 10 minutes, or until almost a glaze.

Meanwhile, melt the butter in a medium saucepan over medium-high heat. Add the flour and cook stirring constantly for 2 minutes or the mixture bubbles and forms a paste. Gradually whisk in the milk, stirring constantly, until the mixture boils. Reduce the heat to low, and cook 2 minutes longer, or until thickened. Add the mustard, cheese, the scallion mixture, and the lobster meat. Bring to a boil. Remove from the heat and place the mixture into the shells. ***Makes 4 servings.***

SHOPPING TIP

Lobster is the king of seafood for its tender, succulent meat. Choose lobsters that are lively in the tank. Lobsters don't eat in captivity, so if they sit too long, they slowly die. Cold-water lobsters are best. When selecting a lobster, touch the shell (make sure the pincers are tied). It should be hard and thick. Soft shells indicate one of two things: that the lobster has recently shed its shell and is growing into a new one (in which case the meat would be skimpy), or that the lobster comes from warm waters.

CRUSTLESS LOBSTER QUICHE

4 teaspoons olive oil, divided

1 medium onion, chopped

1 medium red bell pepper, chopped

8 ounces mushrooms, sliced

2 large eggs

2 large egg whites

1½ cups nonfat cottage cheese

½ cup nonfat plain yogurt

¼ cup all-purpose flour

¼ cup fresh grated Parmesan cheese

⅛ to ¼ teaspoon ground red pepper

¼ teaspoon salt

¼ teaspoon freshly ground black pepper

½ pound lump lobster meat, cooked

½ cup Swiss cheese, shredded

4 scallions, chopped

WINE PAIRING

Pinot Grigio

Preheat the oven to 350°F.

Lightly oil a 10-inch pie plate or quiche dish.

In a large nonstick skillet, heat 2 teaspoons of the oil over medium-high heat. Add the onion and bell pepper and cook, stirring, for 5 minutes, or until softened. Place in a large bowl. Add the remaining 2 teaspoons oil to the skillet and heat over high heat. Add the mushrooms and cook, stirring, until they have softened and most of their liquid has evaporated, for 5 to 7 minutes. Add to the onion mixture.

In a food processor or blender, process the eggs, egg whites, cottage cheese, yogurt, flour, Parmesan cheese, red pepper, salt, and black pepper until smooth. Pour into the bowl with the vegetable mixture. With a rubber spatula, fold in the lobster, Swiss cheese, and scallions. Pour into the prepared baking dish.

Bake for 35 to 45 minutes, or until a knife inserted into the center comes out clean. Let stand for 5 minutes before serving. ***Makes 8 servings.***

COOKING TIP

Cooked lobster may be kept in the refrigerator for up to 3 days. It may also be frozen, but the meat should be picked out of the shell and stored in a zip-top freezer bag for up to a month.

To separate a cooked lobster, hold the tail in one hand and the torso in the other. Twist and pull the tail from the torso. Remove the front legs with the claws. Separate the leg. Pull the small claw away from the large one.

Using a nutcracker or the back of a knife, crack the claw shells and remove the meat.

Wash away any tomalley (green-colored liver of a lobster, considered a delicacy). Using kitchen shears, cut down the underside of the tail.

Bend the shell back and remove the tail meat. Cut a thin slit along the top of the tail to remove the intestinal vein.

STEAMED MUSSELS IN GARLIC-WINE SAUCE

3 pounds mussels, cleaned
(see cooking tip below)

1½ cups white wine

3 cloves garlic, minced, divided

1 medium onion, finely chopped, divided

2 tablespoons olive oil

2 tablespoons chopped fresh parsley leaves

WINE PAIRING

**Sauvignon Blanc
or Pinot Grigio**

30 MINUTES OR LESS

COOKING TIP

Select mussels that snap shut when tapped. This assures that they are alive. Don't buy any mussels with broken shells. Mussels can be stored for up to 2 days in the refrigerator. Place on a tray and cover with a wet towel.

To clean the mussels, use a clam knife or a scouring pad to scrape any barnacles off the shells. Pull off the beardlike strands that stick out through the crack. (This kills the mussels, so cook them immediately.) Place the mussels in a large pot and cover with cool, fresh water by about 2 inches. Agitate the mussels with your hand in a washing-machine motion. Drain and discard the water. Repeat the agitating and draining until the water is clear. Drain and cook.

After cooking mussels, always discard any unopened shells.

In a large saucepan, place the mussels, wine, and about one-quarter of the minced garlic and onion. Bring to a boil over high heat. Cover and steam the mussels for 4 minutes, stirring occasionally, until opened. Discard any unopened mussels. Using a slotted spoon, remove the mussels to a large bowl.

Place a piece of cheesecloth or a coffee filter in a sieve placed over a large bowl. Strain the broth into the bowl.

Wipe the pot clean and add the oil. Heat the oil over medium-high heat. Add the remaining garlic and onion and cook, stirring constantly, for 4 minutes, or until tender. Add the broth. Bring to a boil and cook for 4 minutes, or until reduced slightly and the mixture is opaque. Stir in the parsley. Pour over the mussels and serve. ***Makes 4 servings.***

GOLD MEDAL MARYLAND CRAB CAKES

12 soda crackers, crushed

2 large eggs

2 tablespoons mayonnaise

1 tablespoon Worcestershire sauce

2 teaspoons Old Bay Seasoning

¼ teaspoon ground red pepper

1 pound lump crabmeat

Chardonnay

In a large bowl, combine the crackers, eggs, mayonnaise, Worcestershire sauce, seasoning, and pepper. Stir to combine well.

Pick through the crabmeat to remove any shells. Add the crabmeat to the bowl and toss gently to combine. Shape into 4 cakes.

Heat a nonstick skillet coated with nonstick cooking spray over medium heat. Add the cakes and cook, turning once, for 12 minutes, or until browned and cooked through. ***Makes 4 servings.***

SHOPPING TIP

Crabmeat is sold by grades. Jumbo, lump, or backfin is the best, with large chunks of meat. Flake is smaller pieces of meat.

Crabmeat sold in cans is less desirable than freshly packaged. If purchased in the can, soak the meat in ice water for 10 minutes before using to remove any metallic flavor; drain thoroughly.

CHEF GEORGE'S HOMETOWN PAELLA

3 tablespoons olive oil

1 small onion, minced

1 medium red bell pepper, minced

1 clove garlic, minced

2 cups white rice

2 cups clam juice

1 teaspoon salt

2 pinches saffron threads

1 dozen littleneck clams, soaked overnight

1 dozen mussels, cleaned, beards removed

8 jumbo shrimp, peeled, deveined, and butterflied

8 sea scallops, cut in half

1 pound firm white fish fillet, such as cod, scrod, or monkfish, cut into 8 pieces

10 Spanish olives

WINE PAIRING

Rioja red or white

In a large, deep skillet, heat the oil over medium-high heat. Add the onion, pepper, and garlic and cook, stirring frequently, for 3 minutes. Add the rice and cook for 5 minutes, stirring. Add the clam juice, salt, and 2 cups water and bring to a boil. Reduce the heat to low, cover, and simmer for 20 minutes. Add the saffron, clams, mussels, shrimp, scallops, and fish. Cover and simmer for 5 minutes, stirring occasionally, until the seafood is opaque. Stir in the olives. ***Makes 6 servings.***

FRESH CATCH SEAFOOD LASAGNA

12 lasagna noodles

¼ cup butter

1 medium onion, diced

8 ounces white button mushrooms, sliced

½ pound imitation crabmeat, chopped

½ pound white fish, such as scrod, cod, or whiting, chopped

½ pound peeled and deveined shrimp, chopped

½ pound bay scallops, chopped

¼ cup all-purpose flour

½ teaspoon black pepper

¼ cup dry sherry

1 jar clam juice

1 cup milk

1 cup heavy cream

Salt

1½ cups grated Parmesan cheese, divided

WINE PAIRING

Barbera or Pinot Grigio

Preheat the oven to 350°F.

Coat a 13- × 9-inch baking pan with nonstick cooking spray. Prepare the lasagna noodles according to the package directions.

In a large skillet, melt the butter over medium-high heat. Add the onion and mushrooms and cook for 4 minutes, or until softened and the mushrooms release their liquid.

Add the crabmeat, fish, shrimp, and scallops and cook for 5 minutes, stirring frequently, or until almost opaque. Stir in the flour and pepper and mix well.

Add the sherry and clam juice and stir to release any brown bits. Stir in the milk, cream, and salt to taste and bring to a boil. Boil for 1 minute, or until thickened. Remove from the heat. Stir in 1 cup of the cheese.

Spread 1 cup of the sauce on the bottom of the baking pan. Arrange 3 of the noodles over sauce. Spread 2 cups of the sauce over the noodles. Repeat the layers. Top with the remaining ½ cup of the cheese.

Bake for 35 minutes, or until the top is golden and the sauce is bubbling. Let stand 15 minutes before serving. ***Makes 8 to 12 servings.***

SHOPPING TIP

There are two general types of scallops: bay scallops and sea scallops. Bay scallops are typically found only on the East Coast. Also know as calico scallops, they are very small and sweeter and juicier than sea scallops. Much larger, sea scallops have a sweet, tender meat with a chewier texture than the bay variety.

SWEETS AND TREATS

Right when our customers enter Stew Leonard's, they are greeted by the heady aroma of freshly baked breads, cakes, cookies, and pies. My sister, Beth Leonard Hollis, started our first bakery in our Norwalk store from scratch. Our bakeries are named Bethy's Bakery after her.

There are not too many grocery stores left in the United States that have in-store bakeries, where everything is made from scratch each morning. Each year, the bakeries at Stew Leonard's sell more than 20 times as many baked goods as any other in-store bakery in America. Our bakeries are staffed by the best, most experienced bakers. Just one of our master bakers, Carmine Vartolone, has been making bread for more than 30 years.

Each week, our bakeries sell more than 20,000 loaves of bread, 50,000 muffins, 60,000 bagels, and 250,000 cookies. The recipe for Blue Ribbon Brownies (page 293) is one of our top sellers. Also in this chapter, you'll find delicious pie recipes, such as French-Style Apple Tarte (page 288) and Five-Star Berry Crumb Pie (page 290). During the week of Thanksgiving, we sell more than 40,000 pies.

Many people enjoy fresh fruit for dessert instead of baked goods. So in this chapter, you'll find a bounty of fresh fruit recipes.

Strawberries are such a top seller that we included 10 Winning Ways to WOW Strawberries (page 280) and also one of our chef's specialty recipes, Strawberries with Anisette Cream (page 282).

A great complement to many of these recipes is ice cream. Every Stew Leonard's store has an ice cream parlor that dips soft-serve-style ice cream made fresh every day from the cream Stew's dairy cows produce. The ice cream parlors are open year round and sell an average of 7,000 cones and 3,000 cups per week.

10 Winning Ways to WOW

Strawberries

Traditionally a spring fruit, strawberries are now available year round.

1. SWEET-DIPPED STRAWBERRIES: Start with 1 pint strawberries, ⅓ cup sour cream, and ¼ cup brown sugar, placing each in a separate bowl. Dip the strawberries in the sour cream and then the sugar and eat. A delicious treat! Makes 2 to 4 servings.

2. STRAWBERRY CRISP: Preheat the oven to 375°F. Hull and halve 4 cups strawberries. Place in a buttered 3-quart baking dish or 8-inch square baking pan. In a bowl, using your fingertips, combine ½ cup all-purpose flour, ½ cup packed brown sugar, ½ teaspoon cinnamon, and ⅛ teaspoon salt. Rub in ¼ cup butter until the mixture forms crumbs. Add ½ cup old-fashioned oats and blend just until combined. Sprinkle the crumbs over the berries and bake for 25 minutes, or until bubbling in the center and browned. Makes 6 to 8 servings.

3. CHOCOLATE-COVERED STRAWBERRIES: Clean 12 large strawberries, with stems, with a damp paper towel. Set aside to dry completely. Line a baking sheet with waxed paper. Place 4 ounces milk chocolate chips or semisweet chocolate chips in a small glass bowl with ½ teaspoon vegetable shortening. Place in the microwave and cook on high for 1 to 1½ minutes. Remove and stir the chocolate, stirring to melt any remaining pieces. Holding the berries by the stem, dip ¾ of the berry into the chocolate. Place on the prepared pan to dry. Serve within 24 hours. Makes 12 strawberries.

4. SIMPLE STRAWBERRY SAUCE: Place 1 cup hulled strawberries in a medium bowl with ½ cup sugar. Mash the berries with a fork until smooth. Add 1 cup hulled strawberries, sliced, and ¼ teaspoon cardamom. Toss to coat and let stand for 30 minutes. Serve over ice cream or angel food or pound cake slices. Makes about 1¼ cups.

5. VERY BERRY FRUIT SALAD: In a large bowl, combine 2 tablespoons fresh lemon juice and 1 tablespoon minced crystallized ginger. Add 2 cups hulled and halved strawberries, 2 cups blueberries, and 1 cup raspberries, tossing to coat well. Makes 5 cups.

6. STRAWBERRY SMOOTHIE: In a blender, combine 1 cup hulled and halved strawberries, 1 cup plain yogurt, 2 tablespoons honey, 1 tablespoon frozen orange juice concentrate, and 4 ice cubes. Blend until smooth. Makes 2 servings.

7. FROZEN POPS: In a blender, combine 1 cup hulled and halved strawberries, ½ banana, 1 cup vanilla yogurt, and ½ teaspoon lime zest (optional). Blend until smooth. Pour into frozen pop molds and freeze. Makes 4 to 8 pops.

8. CHOCOLATE STRAWBERRY SHORTCAKE: Preheat the oven to 450°F. Grease a 9-inch round cake pan. Hull and slice 2 pints strawberries. Place in a bowl with ¼ cup sugar, stirring well. Set aside. In a large bowl, combine 1½ cups all-purpose flour, ½ cup unsweetened cocoa powder, ½ cup sugar, and ¼ teaspoon salt. Using a pastry blender, cut in ½ cup butter until the mixture resembles coarse crumbs. Stir in 1 egg, lightly beaten; ⅔ cup milk; and 2 teaspoons vanilla extract, mixing just until blended. Spread into the prepared pan. Bake for 15 minutes, or until a wooden pick inserted in the center of the cake comes out clean. Cool on a rack for 10 minutes. Remove from the pan and cool for 20 minutes. Whip 1 cup heavy cream with 1 tablespoon sugar until soft peaks form. Using a large serrated knife, slice the cake horizontally in half. Place half of the strawberry mixture over the bottom half of the cake. Top with about 1½ cups of the whipped cream. Place the top layer over the whipped cream. Dollop the remaining whipped cream in the center of the cake and drizzle with the remaining strawberries. Makes 8 servings.

9. STRAWBERRIES WITH ANISETTE CREAM: In a heavy saucepan, bring 2 cups milk to a boil. In a small bowl mix together ½ cup sugar, ¼ cup all-purpose flour, and 2 eggs. Remove 1 cup of the milk and gradually whisk the hot milk into the egg mixture. Gradually whisk the egg mixture back into the hot milk. Cook for 5 minutes, stirring constantly, or until the mixture is thickened and coats the back of a spoon. Pour into a large bowl. Cool slightly then cover the surface completely with plastic wrap. Refrigerate the custard for 1 hour, or until cold. Meanwhile place 1 pint stemmed and sliced strawberries, 2 tablespoons sugar, and 2 tablespoons anisette in a small bowl, cover, and refrigerate for 1 hour. Place ½ cup heavy cream in a small bowl. Beat on high for 5 minutes, or until stiff peaks form. Fold the whipped cream and strawberries into the custard. Garnish with whole strawberries and mint sprigs. Makes 4 to 6 servings.

10. STRAWBERRY TART: Thaw 1 sheet puff pastry at room temperature for 30 minutes. Preheat the oven to 400°F. Place the puff pastry on a floured surface and roll into a 12-inch square. Brush the edges with water and fold 1 inch toward the center of the pastry, pressing to seal. Place on a baking sheet and prick the pastry with a fork. Bake for 15 minutes, or until lightly browned. Cool on a wire rack. Spread ½ cup lemon curd over the crust and top with 2 cups strawberries, hulled and halved.

PORT-GLAZED PEACHES

⅓ cup brown sugar

¼ cup tawny port wine

2 tablespoons butter

4 medium peaches, halved lengthwise and pitted

30 MINUTES OR LESS

Preheat the oven to 450°F.

In a 13- × 9-inch baking dish, combine the sugar, wine, and butter. Place in the oven to melt, about 4 minutes. Stir to combine. Place the peaches, cut sides down, in the dish. Bake for 15 minutes, or until tender. Cool in the pan for 10 minutes. Slip the skins off the peaches. Place 2 peach halves on each plate and drizzle with the wine mixture. ***Makes 4 servings.***

COOKING TIP

Serve topped with a dollop of sour cream or whipped cream if desired.

Summer fresh fruit bathed in a flavorful wine sauce is the perfect finale to any meal.

FARM FRESH FRUIT COMPOTE

2 cups dry wine, such as Pinot Grigio

¾ cup sugar

4 whole star anise (optional)

1 tablespoon minced crystallized ginger

4 red plums, quartered and pitted

1 pint black raspberries

1 pint strawberries

In a 3-quart saucepan, combine the wine, sugar, star anise, and ginger. Over medium-high heat, bring to a boil, stirring occasionally. Add the plums and cook for 2 minutes. Remove to a heat-safe glass bowl and stir in the raspberries and strawberries. Cool completely.

Serve at room temperature or chilled. ***Makes 6 to 8 servings.***

COOKING TIP

Beautiful wine glasses can be used for more than just holding our drinks. Here they're filled with a lovely dessert. Why not carry the theme even further by filling extra glasses (champagne flutes work well) with cut flowers such as gerber daisies, lilies, or even roses.

POMEGRANATE-POACHED PEARS

1 bottle (15.2 ounces) pomegranate juice

⅔ cup granulated sugar

1 teaspoon vanilla extract

6 medium firm ripe pears, peeled, halved, and cored

1 cup sour cream

2 tablespoons brown sugar

In a large heavy saucepan, combine the juice, granulated sugar, and vanilla. Bring to a boil, stirring to combine well. Add the pears, reduce the heat to low, cover, and simmer for 15 minutes, or until the pears are just tender when pierced with a knife.

Place the pears in a glass bowl and cool to room temperature. Pour

SHOPPING TIP

Throughout history, the pomegranate has been revered as a symbol of health, fertility, and rebirth. Some cultures also believed it held profound and mystical healing powers. With more antioxidants than red wine or green tea, pomegranates are gaining in popularity, especially with the availability of prepared juice. Not only great in desserts like these poached pears, this flavorful juice can also be used in cocktails or "mocktails."

enough liquid over the pears to cover. When cooled, cover with plastic wrap, and refrigerate for 4 hours or overnight.

Heat the remaining liquid over high heat and cook for 40 minutes, or until thick and syrupy. Remove from the heat and cool to room temperature. Pour the liquid into an airtight container and refrigerate until serving.

Remove the pears from the liquid and discard the poaching liquid.

To serve, in a small bowl, whisk together the sour cream and brown sugar. Place 2 pear halves on 1 of 6 dessert plates. Place a spoonful of the sour cream mixture into the center of each half. Repeat with the remaining pears and sour cream mixture. Drizzle the plates with the poaching syrup. **_Makes 6 servings._**

STORING TIP

Ripen the pears at room temperature. The best ways are to keep them wrapped in the paper they come in or to place them in a paper bag.

FRENCH-STYLE APPLE TARTE

Pastry cream

2 large egg yolks

3 tablespoons sugar

1 tablespoon all-purpose flour

1 tablespoon cornstarch

1 cup whole milk

½ teaspoon vanilla extract

Tart

1 large egg

1 sheet frozen puff pastry, thawed according to package directions

2 medium apples, peeled, cored, and sliced

½ cup apricot preserves

To prepare the pastry cream: In a mixing bowl, with an electric mixer on medium speed, beat the egg yolks and sugar to form ribbons. Mix in the flour and cornstarch.

In a small saucepan, over medium heat, bring the milk to a boil. Remove ½ cup of the milk and gradually whisk the hot milk into the egg mixture. Gradually whisk the egg mixture back into the hot milk. Cook for 5 minutes, stirring constantly, or until the mixture thickens and coats the back of a spoon. Return the mixture to the mixing bowl and mix well. Stir in the vanilla.

Pour into a large bowl. Cool slightly, then cover the surface completely with plastic wrap. Refrigerate the custard for 1 hour or until cold. (Pastry cream may be prepared up to 1 day in advance.)

To prepare the tart: Preheat the oven to 400°F.

In a small bowl, beat the egg with 1 teaspoon water.

Place the puff pastry on a lightly floured cutting board. Cut a 1-inch strip off of each side of the pastry. Using the egg wash, brush a 1-inch border around the edges of the center piece of puff pastry. Place the strips onto the brushed border, folding the corners over to form another layer. Brush the border with the egg wash.

Spoon or pipe the pastry cream onto the center of the puff pastry. Place the apples over the cream and bake for 20 to 25 minutes, or until golden brown and puffed. Remove from the oven and let cool on a rack for 15 minutes.

In a small saucepan, heat the apricot preserves and 3 tablespoons water. Brush onto the apples. Serve warm or refrigerate to serve cold later. *Makes 8 servings.*

FIVE-STAR BERRY CRUMB PIE

Crust

1⅓ cups all-purpose flour

½ teaspoon salt

¼ cup cold butter

¼ cup cold shortening

5 tablespoons ice water

Filling

4 cups strawberries, hulled and halved

2 cups blueberries

1 cup sugar

¼ cup all-purpose flour

1 tablespoon orange juice

Crumb Topping

1⅓ cups all-purpose flour

⅓ cup light brown sugar

⅓ cup pecan halves, chopped

½ teaspoon ground cinnamon

½ cup butter, cut into pieces

To pepare the crust: In a large bowl, combine the flour and salt. Using a pastry blender, cut in the butter and shortening until the mixture resembles coarse crumbs. Stir in the water, 1 tablespoon at a time, until the dough begins to come together. Form the dough into a disk. Wrap in plastic wrap and chill for 15 minutes.

To prepare the filling: Meanwhile, preheat the oven to 425°F.

In a bowl, toss together the strawberries, blueberries, sugar, flour, and orange juice.

To prepare the crumb topping: In a medium bowl, combine the flour, sugar, pecans, and cinnamon. Add the butter and using your hands, work into the flour mixture until crumbs form.

Remove the dough from the refrigerator. On a lightly floured surface, roll the dough to a 12-inch circle. Fit the dough into a 9-inch pie plate. Fold under any overhang and crimp the crust. Place the filling in the crust and top with the crumb topping. Bake for 15 minutes. Reduce the oven temperature to 375°F and bake for 35 minutes longer, or until the center of the pie bubbles.

Cool completely on a rack. ***Makes 8 servings.***

COOKING TIP

For an even easier pie, use a frozen prepared pie crust.

RIPE RASPBERRY COULIS

1 cup fresh raspberries

¼ cup sugar

Place the raspberries and sugar in a saucepan. Bring to a boil, then let stand for 15 minutes. Then puree in a blender or food processor. Strain through a fine strainer.

This sauce is great on cake or ice cream. ***Makes 4 servings.***

STORING TIP

Store berries on a layer of paper towels on a plate or baking sheet. Cover with another dry paper towel. Refrigerate.

Rinse berries just before using by gently running under cool water. Pat dry with paper towels.

To freeze berries, wash and dry them well. Place the berries on a baking sheet lined with waxed paper and freeze for about 2 hours. Once the berries are frozen, transfer them to a zip-top freezer bag. Freeze for up to 9 months.

BLUE RIBBON BROWNIES

½ cup butter

4 ounces unsweetened chocolate

2 cups sugar

4 large eggs

1 tablespoon vanilla extract

½ teaspoon salt

1 cup all-purpose flour

Preheat the oven to 350°F. Grease a 13- × 9-inch baking pan.

Place the butter and chocolate in a large bowl. Cook in the microwave, stirring once, for 4 minutes, or until melted. Remove to the counter and stir in the sugar. Add the eggs, 1 at a time, stirring well after each addition. Stir in the vanilla, salt, and flour. Mix just until blended. Pour into the prepared pan and bake for 30 to 35 minutes, or until a wooden pick inserted in the center comes out clean. ***Makes 16 brownies.***

SHOPPING TIP

Chocolate comes in many varieties and flavors.

If you can see the chocolate you are buying, choose it with shiny color, avoiding white spots. The white spots that form on chocolate are called "bloom" and don't change the flavor. They form from wide variations in storage temperature and although they may look unpleasant, they are fine to eat.

CONNECTICUT'S FAVORITE CHOCOLATE CHIP COOKIES

3½ cups all-purpose flour

2 teaspoons baking soda

1 teaspoon salt

1¼ cups margarine or butter

1 cup granulated sugar

1 cup packed light brown sugar

2 large eggs

1 teaspoon vanilla extract

1½ tablespoons corn syrup (optional)

1 bag (12 ounces) chocolate chips

Preheat the oven to 375°F.

In a medium bowl, whisk together the flour, baking soda, and salt.

In a large bowl, with an electric mixer at medium speed, beat the margarine or butter with the sugars until light and fluffy. Add the eggs, vanilla, and corn syrup, if using. Beat until smooth. Beat in the flour mixture until combined. Stir in the chocolate chips.

Drop by teaspoonfuls onto a baking sheet. Bake for 10 minutes, or until browned and risen. Cool on the pan for 2 minutes. Remove to a rack to cool completely. ***Makes about 36 cookies.***

These cookies were voted the best chocolate chip cookie in Connecticut by Connecticut magazine readers. We make them with margarine because taste tests have proven our customers prefer them prepared with margarine more than with butter.

COOKING TIP

For Chocolate Chocolate Chip Cookies as shown in the picture, add $\frac{1}{3}$ cup unsweetened cocoa powder to the flour mixture.

Christopher lived briefly in Norwalk, Connecticut, while young and remembers his mother always taking him to Stew Leonard's to get an ice cream cone and listen to the puppets sing in the store. Now a financial planner, Chris lives in Madison, Connecticut, although he still makes trips to Stew Leonard's because the food is always fresh, and they have the best meats.

Chris entered the recipe contest on a whim when he saw entry forms in the Stew Leonard's Wine Shop. He submitted a recipe that his grandmother and mother used to make, always a family favorite.

CHRISTOPHER GAVIN'S
CREAM CHEESE-CHOCOLATE CHIP COOKIES

1 package (8 ounces) cream cheese

2 large eggs

½ cup sugar

2 tubes (19 ounces) refrigerated chocolate chip cookie dough, each cut into slices

Preheat the oven to 350°F.

In a medium bowl, with an electric mixer set on low speed, blend the cream cheese, eggs, and sugar until well blended.

Arrange half of the cookie slices on the bottom of a 13- × 9-inch baking pan, pressing to form a sheet. Spread the cream cheese mixture over the cookies. Top with the remaining sliced cookies.

Bake the cookies for 25 to 30 minutes, or until lightly browned. Cool on a rack. Serve warmed or cool. ***Makes 24 cookies.***

DOUBLE CHOCOLATE BROWNIE COOKIES

8 ounces semisweet chocolate

4 ounces (1 stick) butter

1 cup sugar

3 large eggs

2 teaspoons vanilla extract

¼ teaspoon salt

1 teaspoon baking powder

1¼ cups all-purpose flour

1 bag (12 ounces) milk chocolate chips

1 cup walnuts, chopped

Preheat the oven to 350°F.

Place the semisweet chocolate in a large bowl. Microwave for 2 minutes. Stir. Cook for another 1 to 2 minutes, or until the chocolate is almost melted. Stir. Set aside to cool slightly. In a large bowl, with an electric mixer on low speed, combine the butter and sugar. Increase the speed to medium and beat for 4 minutes, or until light and fluffy. Add the melted chocolate, eggs, vanilla, salt, and baking powder. Beat on low for 1 minute. Increase the speed to medium and beat for 3 minutes, or until well blended, occasionally scraping the sides of the bowl. Add the flour and beat on low for 1 minute, or until well blended. Stir in the chocolate chips and walnuts.

Drop by teaspoonfuls onto a baking sheet. Bake for 10 minutes, or until browned. Cool on the baking sheet for 2 minutes. Remove to a rack to cool completely. ***Makes 48 cookies.***

GRANDMA'S OATMEAL-RAISIN COOKIES

8 ounces (2 sticks) butter

1 cup granulated sugar

1 cup packed light brown sugar

2 large eggs

1 teaspoon vanilla extract

1 teaspoon baking powder

½ teaspoon salt

3 cups oats

1½ cups all-purpose flour

½ cup raisins

½ cup chopped walnuts

Preheat the oven to 350°F.

In a large bowl, with an electric mixer on low speed, combine the butter, granulated sugar, and brown sugar. Increase the speed to medium and beat for 4 minutes, or until light and fluffy. Add the eggs, vanilla, baking powder, and salt. Beat on low for 1 minute. Increase the speed to medium and beat for 3 minutes, or until well blended, occasionally scraping the sides of the bowl. Add the oats and flour and beat on low for 1 minute, or until well blended. Stir in the raisins and walnuts.

Drop by teaspoonfuls onto a baking sheet. Bake for 10 minutes, or until browned. Cool on the baking sheet for 2 minutes. Remove to a rack to cool completely. ***Makes 48 cookies.***

COUNTRY FAIR RASPBERRY BLONDIES

2 cups all-purpose flour

1 teaspoon baking powder

½ teaspoon salt

¼ teaspoon baking soda

2 cups packed light brown sugar

¾ cup butter, at room temperature

2 large eggs

1 tablespoon vanilla extract

1 cup chocolate chips

½ pint raspberries

Preheat the oven to 350°F. Grease a 13- × 9-inch baking pan.

In a medium bowl, whisk together the flour, baking powder, salt, and baking soda.

In a large bowl, with an electric mixer on medium-high speed, beat the sugar and butter until light and creamy. Add the eggs, 1 at a time, until fluffy. Beat in the vanilla. Add the flour mixture and beat on low speed, just until combined.

Stir in the chocolate chips.

Spread the batter into the prepared pan and place the raspberries on top of the batter. Bake for 50 minutes, or until a wooden pick inserted in the center comes out clean. Cool completely in the pan on a rack. Cut into 12 pieces and serve. ***Makes 12 servings.***

FLOURLESS CHOCOLATE CAKE

12 ounces semisweet chocolate

¾ cup butter

6 large eggs, separated and at room temperature

1 tablespoon vanilla extract

1 tablespoon instant espresso

⅓ cup sugar

Whipped cream for garnish

Preheat the oven to 350°F. Butter a 9-inch springform pan. Wrap the outside of the pan securely in foil.

Place the chocolate and butter in a large microwave-safe bowl. Cook in the microwave on medium-high for 3 to 5 minutes, stirring frequently until melted. Cool slightly. Whisk in the egg yolks, vanilla, and espresso, stirring until smooth.

In another large mixing bowl, with a mixer set on high speed, beat the egg whites until foamy. Gradually add the sugar and beat until stiff, glossy peaks form. Stir one-third of the egg whites into the chocolate mixture. Whisk in the remaining egg whites, half of the mixture at a time. Pour the mixture into the prepared pan and bake for 45 to 50 minutes, or until the top is puffed and a wooden pick inserted in the center comes out with a few crumbs.

Cool completely on a rack. Remove the sides of the pan and slide the cake onto a serving plate. Garnish with the whipped cream. ***Makes 10 to 12 servings.***

BANANA CAKE WITH FRESH RASPBERRIES

Cake

1¾ cups all-purpose flour plus 1 tablespoon

1 teaspoon baking soda

½ teaspoon salt

1 cup raspberries

1 cup packed light brown sugar

½ cup butter

1 cup mashed ripe banana (about 2 bananas)

2 large eggs

2 teaspoons vanilla extract

½ cup buttermilk

Frosting

½ cup butter, at room temperature

1 package (8 ounces) cream cheese, at room temperature

4 cups confectioners' sugar

1 to 4 tablespoons milk

Raspberries for garnish

Mint sprigs for garnish

Preheat the oven to 350°F. Grease and flour an 8-inch square baking pan.

To prepare the cake: In a small bowl, whisk together the 1¾ cups flour, baking soda, and salt. In another small bowl, toss the raspberries with the remaining 1 tablespoon flour. Set both aside.

This rich banana cake is studded with fresh raspberries. Topped with a cream cheese frosting, it's a delightful dessert.

In a large bowl, with an electric mixer on medium speed, cream the sugar and butter until light and fluffy. Add the banana, eggs, and vanilla and beat well. Add the flour mixture and beat slowly while adding the buttermilk, beating just until blended. Fold in the raspberries.

Spread into the prepared pan and bake for 45 minutes, or until a wooden pick inserted in the center of the pan comes out clean. Place the pan on a rack and cool for 5 minutes. Remove the cake from the pan and cool completely.

To prepare the frosting: Meanwhile, in a medium bowl, with an electric mixer on low speed, beat the butter and cream cheese until light and creamy. Add the confectioners' sugar and 1 tablespoon of the milk and beat on low until blended, adding more milk if necessary.

To assemble the cake, cut the cake horizontally in half. Place the bottom layer of the cake, cut side up, on a cake plate. Spread 1 cup of the frosting onto the cake layer. Place the top layer of the cake, cut side down, onto the cake. Spread the remaining frosting on the top and sides of the cake. Garnish with the raspberries and mint sprigs. ***Makes 12 servings.***

COOKING TIP

To reduce the fat slightly in this cake, use reduced-fat cream cheese.

PORT WINE CAKE

1¼ cups sugar, divided

½ cup butter, at room temperature

3 large eggs

2 teaspoons vanilla extract

½ teaspoon orange zest

2 cups all-purpose flour

1½ teaspoons baking powder

½ teaspoon salt

⅓ cup ruby port wine

½ cup orange preserves

Preheat the oven to 350°F. Butter an 8-inch round or 8-inch square cake pan. Sprinkle 1 tablespoon of the sugar in the pan, tossing to coat the butter with the sugar.

COOKING TIP

Zest adds a fresh citrus flavor to dishes both sweet and savory. It is the thin, brightly colored part a citrus fruit's skin.

To zest a fruit, always wash and dry the fruit. Using a zester, rasp, or the fine side of a box grater, rub the fruit just until the color is gone and you see the white pith.

In a large bowl, with an electric mixer on medium speed, beat the remaining sugar with the butter until fluffy. Add the eggs, vanilla, and orange zest and beat for 1 minute.

Add the flour, baking powder, and salt and beat for 3 minutes. Remove 1 cup of the batter and place in a small bowl. Pour the remaining batter into the prepared pan.

Stir the port wine into the batter in the bowl. Drop the batter by spoonfuls onto the batter in the pan. Swirl with a butter knife.

Bake the cake for 30 minutes, or until a wooden pick inserted in the center comes out clean.

Place the pan on a rack and cool for 15 minutes. Remove the cake from the pan to the rack and cool completely.

Place the preserves in a small saucepan and heat over low heat until melted. Brush onto the top of the cake. ***Makes 8 to 10 servings.***

COOKING TIP

For a lovely presentation, bake this cake in a 6-cup Bundt pan. Dust with confectioners' sugar before serving.

Stacey said, "I have been shopping at Stew's since I moved here from Long Island 9 years ago. I love Stew's—the selection, the freshness of the items. And I am always amazed when I get to the register and the total is less than I was expecting for the quality and quantity of things that I bought. I saw this contest online—I receive the Stew Leonard's e-mail newsletter—and I though it would be fun to enter my recipe!

"Several years ago, my mother and I went on a cooking trip to Italy. Two girls came every night to the old farmhouse we were staying in, and we helped cook dinner with them. They taught us how to make tiramisu, but I had to make some alterations when I returned home. They didn't have the same ingredients here, and the girls who were teaching us never gave us very exact measurements or instructions! It's a favorite in our household now."

Stacey has been married for 10 years and is a stay-at-home mom to three children.

STACEY LLOYD'S
TIRAMISU

4 large eggs, separated

4 tablespoons sugar

1 pound mascarpone cheese

Splash brandy

1 cup strong coffee or espresso

Pavesini or Savoiardi Italian Biscuits

Bittersweet baking chocolate, grated

In a bowl, beat the egg yolks with the sugar until they look white.

In a separate bowl, whip the egg whites until soft peaks form. Fold the cheese softly into the egg yolk mixture, then fold into the egg whites.

In a third bowl, combine the brandy and coffee or espresso. Wet the biscuits with the brandy mixture. Place a layer of the biscuits on the bottom of an 8-inch glass baking dish or a 2-quart shallow bowl. Then add half of the cheese mixture, then another layer of biscuits, then the rest of the cheese mixture. (If the bowl is glass, put some of the biscuits along the sides as well.)

Refrigerate the biscuits for at least 1 hour, or until set. Sprinkle with the chocolate. ***Makes 8 to 10 servings.***

ELEGANT CHOCOLATE MOUSSE

1 cup chocolate chips

¼ cup butter

3 large egg yolks

¾ cup sugar, divided

4 cups heavy cream

2 tablespoons cocoa powder

Place the chocolate chips and butter in a large glass bowl. Microwave for 1 minute. Stir the mixture and microwave for 30 seconds longer, or until just melted.

Place the egg yolks in a double boiler with ½ cup of the sugar. Heat to 165°F, stirring frequently. Remove from the heat and with an electric mixer, beat until light in color and the mixture doubles in volume and forms ribbons. Fold into the chocolate mixture.

Place the cream and the remaining ¼ cup sugar in a large mixing bowl. With an electric mixer on medium-high speed, beat until stiff peaks form.

Stir about 1 cup of the whipped cream and the cocoa powder into the chocolate mixture. Fold in the remaining whipped cream. ***Makes 8 to 12 servings.***

HEAVENLY AMBROSIA

2 cans (4 ounces each) diced peaches

1 can (11 ounces) mandarin oranges

1 can (8 ounces) pineapple tidbits

1 container (8 ounces) sour cream

1 cup mini marshmallows

½ cup shredded coconut

½ cup green grapes

½ cup red grapes

Place a colander in the sink. Drain the peaches, oranges, and pineapple in the colander.

In a large bowl, combine the sour cream, marshmallows, and coconut until well blended. Add the grapes and drained fruit, gently tossing to coat well.

Refrigerate if not serving immediately. ***Makes 8 servings.***

COOKING TIP

This item is a favorite one from the Stew Leonard's salad bar. For a lower calorie version, eliminate the marshmallows and use unsweetened coconut instead.

WALNUT CRÈME WITH FRESH FRUIT

1 tablespoon butter

¼ cup sugar

¼ cup toasted walnuts, ground

1 teaspoon walnut oil

1 pinch salt

1 cup heavy cream

Assorted cut fruit

In a small skillet, melt the butter over medium heat. Add the sugar and cook until dissolved. Stir in the walnuts, walnut oil, and salt. Remove from the heat and set aside to cool.

Place the cream in a large bowl. With an electric mixer on high speed, beat until stiff peaks form. Fold the walnut mixture into the cream. Serve over the fruit or alongside a fruit pie or tart. ***Makes 2½ cups.***

CRÈME ANGLAISE FRENCH CUSTARD SAUCE

6 large egg yolks

1 cup sugar

2 cups milk

1 vanilla bean, halved lengthwise

In a small bowl, whisk together the egg yolks and sugar.

Place the milk and the vanilla bean in a medium saucepan. Bring just to a boil over medium heat.

Remove 1 cup of the milk and gradually whisk the hot milk into the egg mixture. Gradually whisk the egg mixture back into the hot milk. Cook for 5 minutes, stirring constantly, or until the mixture thickens and coats the back of a spoon. Return the mixture to the mixing bowl and mix well. Strain the mixture into a bowl. Cover and refrigerate for 2 hours or up to 1 day. ***Makes 4 cups.***

COOKING TIP

Serve the cream with a chocolate cake, pie, or tart.

BREAKFASTS AND BRUNCHES

Perhaps it's unusual to end our recipes with breakfasts, but it's the most important meal of the day after all! Breakfast and brunch foods are popular at my home. After every busy holiday, I cook up my secret egg sandwich recipe to serve to all our 2,000 Team Members as one way to thank them for working so hard.

In this chapter, you'll find both baked goods breakfast foods—such as Low Country Corn Muffins (page 326), Bethy's Blueberry Muffins (page 324), and Deep Chocolate-Cherry Bread (page 320)—and also hearty egg-based dishes, including Baked Eggs with Vegetable Ragout (page 328), Goat Cheese Scrambled Eggs (page 331), and Fall Baked French Toast with Pears and Pecans (page 332).

At Stew Leonard's, we get all of our eggs from local farmers. They're the freshest, best eggs available. Over the past few years, organic eggs have become very popular, and we stock them in our stores with pride.

Quite a few of the recipes in this chapter rely on milk. My family has been bottling milk since 1921, way back when my grandfather Charles Leo Leonard delivered it to families by horse and wagon. Today our milk comes from our dairy farm in Ellington, Connecticut, where more than 1,000 cows work hard to produce milk for our stores. Our farmers feed our cows an all-natural diet of hay, malted barley, grain, corn, soybeans, and canola. The cows are milked each morning, and the milk is immediately delivered to our in-store dairy plant in Norwalk. With our unique pasteurization recipe developed by my grandfather, we take special care to use high heat that caramelizes the natural sugars in the milk during pasteurization. This gives our milk a taste like no other. The milk is then processed and packaged immediately for sale on our shelves. Customers can buy milk that has gone from farm to shelf in as little as 6 hours.

10 Winning Ways to WOW

Coffee

There's nothing better than a hot cup of fresh brewed coffee to start your day. But when you are looking to spice up your morning drink, whether for guests or just yourself, these delicious versions of Stew Leonard's favorite breakfast drink will do the trick.

1. IRISH COFFEE: Warm a stemmed coffee glass or coffee mug. Add 1 shot of Irish whiskey and 1 teaspoon sugar. Fill the mug two-thirds full with hot brewed coffee. Top with heavy or whipped cream.

2. EGGNOG COFFEE: Brew a pot of strong rich coffee (flavored coffees work great). Meanwhile, place an equal amount of prepared eggnog in a saucepan. Bring to a simmer. Place a cinnamon stick in each coffee mug. Pour equal portions of coffee and eggnog into each. Top each with a dollop of whipped cream.

3. CHAI SPICED COFFEE: Prepare a pot of strong French roast coffee and add a pinch of cinnamon, nutmeg, and cardamom to the grounds before brewing. Place 2 tablespoons sweetened condensed milk into each mug and fill with the brewed coffee.

4. PERFECT ICED COFFEE: Double the amount of the coffee (but not the water) that you would use for hot coffee. Brew as you would hot coffee. Let cool for a few minutes. Fill a temperature-safe pitcher with ice cubes and pour the coffee over the ice. Serve with half-and-half or milk and sugar to taste. Cover and refrigerate any remaining coffee.

5. COFFEE SPRITZER: Make a pot of coffee as for Iced Coffee. Set aside to cool

for a moment and sweeten the coffee if desired. Fill a glass with ice cubes. Pour the coffee into the glass to half full. Top with seltzer water or club soda.

6. COLA ICE-CREAM FLOAT: Place ½ cup Iced Coffee in a tall glass. Add 1 scoop coffee ice cream. Pour ½ cup cola soda over the float.

7. CAFÉ MOCHA SHAKE: Place 1 cup cooled strong coffee and 1 cup cold milk in a blender. Add 1 cup chocolate ice cream and 1 tablespoon chocolate syrup or sauce. Blend until smooth.

8. CHOCOLATE-COVERED COFFEE BEANS: Melt 4 ounces good-quality chocolate (such as bittersweet, milk, or white). Add 1 cup coffee beans, tossing to coat. Using a fork, remove the beans from the chocolate and place them on a piece of waxed paper, being sure to separate. Set aside to let dry completely. These are especially good with flavored coffee beans.

9. RICH CHOCOLATE DESSERTS: Add 1 tablespoon finely ground espresso or rich coffee to chocolate cakes, brownies, or cookies. The coffee heightens the chocolate flavor.

10. COFFEE GRANITA: In a large bowl, combine 4 cups hot strong brewed coffee, 1 cup sugar, and 2 teaspoons vanilla extract. Stir well until the sugar dissolves. Refrigerate for 2 hours, or until cooled. Add 1 tablespoon coffee liqueur, such as Kahlúa. Place in a 13- × 9-inch metal pan. Freeze for 1 hour, or until the mixture becomes icy at the edge of the pan. Stir with a fork to distribute the icy portion into the liquid. Freeze again for 45 minutes and stir as before. Freeze for 3 hours, or until solid. Using a fork, scrape the granita in long strokes, forming flakes. Freeze for 1 hour. Serve in glass dishes or wineglasses with a dollop of whipped cream.

CHERRY-CITRUS TEA SCONES

1 large egg

½ cup half-and-half or whole milk plus
2 tablespoons, divided

½ teaspoon orange zest

2 cups all-purpose flour

3 tablespoons sugar

1 tablespoon baking powder

½ teaspoon salt

¼ cup butter, cut into pieces

1 cup cherries, pitted, cut into quarters and patted dry

Preheat the oven to 425°F.

In a small bowl, whisk together the egg, ½ cup of the half-and-half or milk, and the orange zest.

In a large bowl, whisk together the flour, sugar, baking powder, and salt. Add the butter and using a pastry blender or 2 knives, cut the butter into the flour mixture until it resembles coarse crumbs.

Make a well in the center of the flour mixture and add the egg mixture. Stir just until blended. With your hands, knead in the cherries. Place on a lightly floured surface and knead for 1 minute. Pat into an 8-inch circle. Cut into 12 wedges and place on an ungreased baking sheet at least ½ inch apart. Brush the tops with the remaining 2 tablespoons half-and-half or milk.

Bake for 12 to 15 minutes, or until golden brown. Place on a rack to cool.
Makes 12 servings.

THE PERFECT BREW

When you come around the first aisle at Stew Leonard's, you're greeted by the aroma of freshly brewed coffee. There's a Stew Leonard's Coffee Bar in each of our stores, and they all bustle every morning with customers stopping in on their way to work. Cappuccino is one of our best sellers, and it's one of my favorite beverages, too.

We import our coffee beans directly from the best coffee plantations in the mountainous terrains around the equator. Coffee is very perishable, so at Stew Leonard's we roast and grind our coffee each day. We use about a dozen types of beans from around the world. We offer more than 40 different roasts, blends, and flavors. The strongest blends are Stew's Choice, Café du Jour, and French Roast, but Hazelnut is by far our best-selling coffee.

If you're making cappuccino at home, start with fresh beans. Coffee experts recommend buying whole beans and grinding them right before brewing. If possible, buy beans within 2 to 3 days of roasting and purchase no more beans than you'll drink within a week. Store your coffee beans in a tightly sealed bag, tucked into an airtight opaque container, placed in a cool spot away from the stove.

You don't need an expensive cappuccino machine to make delicious foamy cappuccino. This simple method requires only a blender or food processor.

STEW LEONARD'S CAPPUCCINO

1 cup skim or whole milk

4 cups strong, freshly brewed coffee or espresso

Ground cinnamon or cocoa powder

Place the milk in a saucepan over high heat. Heat the milk just until it begins to boil. Pour the hot milk into a blender or food processor. Blend the milk for 1 minute, until foamy. Fill four mugs two-thirds full with coffee. Top each with some milk foam and a pinch of cinnamon or cocoa powder. Enjoy! *Makes 4 servings.*

DEEP CHOCOLATE-CHERRY BREAD

3¼ to 3¾ cups all-purpose flour, divided

⅓ cup unsweetened cocoa powder

2 packages (¼ ounce each) instant (rapid-rise) yeast

1 teaspoon salt

⅓ cup honey

½ cup butter, cut up

1 teaspoon vanilla extract

⅓ cup semisweet chocolate morsels

⅓ cup dried cherries

In a large mixing bowl, combine 1 cup of the flour, the cocoa powder, the undissolved yeast, and the salt.

COOKING TIP

Instant or rapid-rise yeast will save you time and energy when baking. Using this exceptional product eliminates the need for two periods of rising, cutting the time by hours.

In a small saucepan, heat 1 cup water and the honey and butter until warm (120° to 130°F). Gradually add to the dry ingredients and using an electric mixer with a dough hook attached, on medium speed, beat for 2 minutes, scraping the bowl occasionally. Add the vanilla and ½ cup of the flour and beat on high speed for 2 minutes, scraping the bowl occasionally. With a spoon, stir in enough of the remaining flour to make a soft dough.

Knead on a lightly floured surface for about 4 to 6 minutes, or until smooth and elastic. Cover and let rest for 10 minutes.

Knead the chocolate morsels and the cherries into the dough. Shape into a long loaf about 12 inches long and place on a baking sheet. Cover and let rise in a warm, draft-free place for about 45 minutes, or until doubled in size.

Preheat the oven to 350°F.

Bake for 45 to 50 minutes, or until the bread sounds hollow when tapped, covering with foil if necessary after 20 minutes to prevent excess browning. Remove to a wire rack. Cool completely. ***Makes 1 loaf.***

SHOPPING TIP

Store chocolate in a zip-top plastic bag or in plastic wrap in a cool, dry place for up to 1 year.

Nancy has been a Stew Leonard's shopper since 1990. Her first visit was to the Norwalk store to buy oatmeal-raisin cookies (which her then-boyfriend, now husband, raved about!).

Nancy entered the Cook-Off at her husband's suggestion. "I love to cook and bake for my family and friends," said Nancy. "We frequently entertain and love to prepare food, both proven favorites and new dishes, for our guests. I have also participated in several local baking contests over the last few years and won prizes."

The inspiration for Nancy's recipe was her grandmother's cinnamon-raisin bread pudding plus her husband's love of coconut. After several attempts and a lot of tasting, Nancy came up with the Coconut Bread Pudding with Dried Apricots version.

NANCY DUNN'S

COCONUT BREAD PUDDING WITH DRIED APRICOTS

1 large loaf firm white or Italian bread (1 pound), crusts trimmed, cut into 1-inch cubes

¾ cup sweetened shredded coconut

⅓ cup dried apricots, thinly sliced (about 2 ounces)

2½ cups canned cream of coconut, such as Coco Lopez

2 cups whole milk

½ cup sugar

1 tablespoon vanilla extract

6 large eggs

Preheat the oven to 350°F.

Arrange half of the bread cubes in a 13- × 9- × 2-inch glass baking dish. Sprinkle with half of the shredded coconut and all of the apricots. Layer with the remaining bread cubes and coconut.

Combine the cream of coconut, milk, sugar, and vanilla in a heavy large saucepan. Cook over medium heat, stirring frequently, until the sugar dissolves and the mixture is just warm. Remove from the heat. Whisk together the eggs in a large bowl. Remove 1 cup of the warm mixture from the pan and whisk into the bowl with the eggs. Whisk the egg mixture into the warm milk mixture. Pour the mixture over the bread in a baking dish. Using the back of a spoon, push the bread gently into the milk mixture. Let stand for 15 minutes. Bake for 50 minutes, or until the pudding is set and golden brown. Place on a rack and cool slightly. Serve warm sprinkled with confectioners' sugar or topped with whipped cream if desired. ***Makes 10 servings.***

BETHY'S BLUEBERRY MUFFINS

1¾ cups all-purpose flour

1½ teaspoons baking powder

1 teaspoon salt

6 tablespoons butter, melted

¾ cup sugar

2 large eggs

¾ cup milk

1 cup fresh or frozen blueberries

Preheat the oven to 400°F. Grease 12 muffin cups or line 12 muffin cups with paper cupcake liners.

In a small bowl, whisk together the flour, baking powder, and salt.

SHOPPING TIP

Wild blueberries are tiny berries that grow naturally in the Northeast region of North America. They are actually wild—not planted like cultivated blueberries, the larger and more common ones. Because of their concentrated deep-blue pigments, they contain more of the antioxidant phytochemicals anthocyanin and phenolics than their cultivated cousins. But don't let their size fool you; these tiny fruits are loaded with flavor. Look for wild blueberries in the freezer section of the supermarket for year-round enjoyment.

Fresh blueberries stud these delicious muffins, which are a favorite in Stew Leonard's bakery.

In a large bowl, stir together the butter, sugar, and eggs until combined. Add the flour mixture and the milk and stir just until blended. Stir in the blueberries just until blended. Evenly divide the batter between the muffin cups.

Bake for 12 to 16 minutes, or until a wooden pick inserted in the center comes out clean. ***Makes 12 servings.***

LOW COUNTRY CORN MUFFINS

¾ cup milk

⅓ cup vegetable oil

1 large egg

1½ cups all-purpose flour

1 cup cornmeal

¾ cup sugar

2 teaspoons baking powder

½ teaspoon salt

Preheat the oven to 375°F. Grease 12 muffin cups or line 12 muffin cups with paper cupcake liners.

In a measuring cup, whisk together the milk, oil, and egg.

In a large bowl, whisk together the flour, cornmeal, sugar, baking powder, and salt. Make a well in the center of the flour mixture and add the milk mixture. Stir just until blended. Evenly divide the batter between the muffin cups.

Bake for 12 to 20 minutes, or until a wooden pick inserted in the center comes out clean. ***Makes 12 servings.***

COOKING TIP

Add your favorite berry to these muffins for an exciting sweet flavor. Simply toss 1 cup blueberries, raspberries, or blackberries with 1 tablespoon flour before gently tossing into the mixture. Or, for a savory variety, add ½ cup shredded cheese, such as sharp Cheddar or Monterey Jack with jalapeños.

HASH BROWNS

2 tablespoons butter

1 large onion, chopped

4 leftover baked potatoes, peeled and cut into ½-inch pieces

1 teaspoon salt

½ teaspoon ground black pepper

2 tablespoons chopped parsley

Melt the butter in a large skillet over medium-high heat. Add the onion, potatoes, salt, and pepper and cook for 5 minutes without stirring. Turn the potatoes and cook for 10 minutes longer, or until tender and well browned.

Stir in the parsley. ***Makes 6 to 8 servings.***

BAKED EGGS WITH VEGETABLE RAGOUT

2 tablespoons olive oil

1 medium red onion, chopped

1 medium red bell pepper, chopped

1 medium yellow bell pepper, chopped

1 small zucchini, chopped

2 cloves garlic, minced

2 plum tomatoes, seeded and chopped

2 tablespoons chopped fresh thyme or rosemary

½ teaspoon salt

6 large eggs

Salt

Ground black pepper

30 MINUTES OR LESS

Preheat the oven to 400°F. Grease 6 six-ounce ramekins. Place the ramekins in a large baking pan. Bring 4 cups water to a boil.

Meanwhile, heat the oil in a large skillet over medium-high heat. Add the onion, bell peppers, and zucchini and cook for 5 minutes, or until almost tender. Add the garlic and cook for 1 minute. Stir in the tomatoes, thyme or rosemary, and salt. Cook for 3 minutes, or until well blended.

Evenly divide the vegetable mixture into the ramekins. Break 1 egg into each ramekin and sprinkle each with a pinch of salt and black pepper. Pour the boiling water around the ramekins in the pan and carefully place the pan in the oven. Bake for 10 to 12 minutes, or until the whites of the egg are firm and the yolks are just starting to set. ***Makes 6 servings.***

FLORENTINE QUICHE

4 slices bacon, cut into ½-inch pieces

1 small onion, finely chopped

4 cups baby spinach leaves

8 large eggs

1½ cups milk

¼ teaspoon ground black pepper

4 ounces Jarlsberg or Gruyère cheese, shredded
(about 1 cup)

Preheat the oven to 375°F. Grease a 10-inch quiche pan or pie plate.

In a large skillet over medium heat, cook the bacon for 5 minutes, or until browned. Remove with a slotted spoon to paper towels. Remove and discard all but 2 tablespoons of the drippings. Cook the onion in the drippings, stirring for 4 minutes, or until tender. Add the spinach and cook, stirring, for 2 minutes. Place in the prepared pan.

In a large bowl, whisk together the eggs, milk, pepper, cheese, and bacon. Pour in the pan. Bake for 35 minutes, or until the filling is set and puffed slightly. Let stand for 10 minutes before serving. ***Makes 6 to 8 servings.***

COOKING TIP

This dish is a favorite take-out dish at Stew Leonard's and is sure to please everyone at the table whether they are watching their weight or not. Serve it with whole grain toast and melon slices.

Creamy scrambled eggs and Hash Browns (page 327) make for delicious, yet simple brunch fare.

GOAT CHEESE SCRAMBLED EGGS

8 large eggs

2 tablespoons chopped chives

¼ teaspoon salt

¼ teaspoon ground black pepper

2 tablespoons butter

4 ounces goat cheese, crumbled

In a large bowl, whisk together the eggs, 2 tablespoons water, chives, salt, and pepper.

Melt the butter in a large skillet over medium-high heat. Add the egg mixture and cook, stirring frequently, until almost set. Add the goat cheese and cook, stirring, until the eggs are just set and the cheese is melted. ***Makes 4 servings.***

The flavor of goat cheese varies widely according to its age and the way it is made. Domestic cheeses tend to be more moist and mild tasting. The French cheeses have a more pronounced tartness. To judge the freshness of goat cheese, pick it up and squeeze slightly. If it is very soft, it is fresh and subtle tasting; if the cheese feels firm and bounces back a little, it is older and a bit more tart. If it is very hard, put it back; it is probably too old.

FALL BAKED FRENCH TOAST WITH PEARS AND PECANS

6 large eggs

1 cup half-and-half or milk

2 tablespoons honey

2 teaspoons vanilla extract

½ teaspoon salt

8 thick slices bread, such as country hearth bread, whole grain, semolina, challah, or country white

2 tablespoons butter

2 medium ripe pears, peeled and sliced

¼ cup maple syrup

¼ cup pecan halves, toasted (see page 32)

Coat a 13- × 9-inch glass baking dish with cooking spray.

In a large bowl, whisk together the eggs, half-and-half or milk, honey, vanilla, and salt. Pour into the prepared dish. Add the bread slices to the dish, turning to coat with the egg mixture. Arrange the slices in the dish so that they fit together and are covered with the egg mixture. Cover with plastic wrap, pressing the bread slices down into the egg mixture. Refrigerate overnight.

Bring the dish to room temperature. Preheat the oven to 350°F.

Bake the French toast for 25 to 35 minutes, or until puffed and well browned.

Fresh fruit bathes tender slices of French toast. For summertime French toast, try fresh peaches, plums, or apricots in place of the pears.

Meanwhile, melt the butter in a skillet over medium-high heat. Add the pears and cook, stirring gently, until golden brown. Add the syrup and cook for 5 minutes, or until hot.

Remove the French toast from the oven and top with the pear-syrup mixture. Sprinkle with the pecans and serve. ***Makes 4 to 6 servings.***

COOKING TIP

For a lovely brunch, serve this tasty dish with mimosas. Combine equal parts orange juice and champagne and place in champagne flutes.

The vibrant red, white, and blue colors of this salad make it a perfect Fourth of July offering.
Fresh fruits come to life with the simple addition of lime or lemon juice and fresh mint.

ALL-AMERICAN FRUIT SALAD

5 cups cubed watermelon

1 pint blueberries

3 tablespoons chopped fresh mint

1 tablespoon fresh lime or lemon juice

2 large bananas, peeled and sliced

1 medium star fruit, sliced, for garnish

In a large bowl, toss together the watermelon, blueberries, mint, and lime or lemon juice. Toss to coat well and let stand for at least 30 minutes, or cover and refrigerate for 2 hours.

Just before serving, add the banana slices and garnish with the star fruit. ***Makes 8 servings.***

SHOPPING TIP

Melons are a summer classic, with cantaloupe, honeydew, and watermelon leading the list of favorites.

Choose heavy melons with smooth, firm skin.

Menus for All Occasions

Super Bowl

Easy Italian Chicken Wings 41

Fresh Fried Mozzarella with Pesto 36

Three-Cheese Mini Calzones 26

Fix-It-Fast Grilled Vegetable Hoagie 126

Blue Ribbon Brownies 293

Country Fair Raspberry Blondies 300

Romantic Dinner

Mesclun Salad with Pears and Stilton 55

Filet Mignon with Cognac-Peppercorn Sauce 134

Caramelized Onion Mashed Potatoes 95

Holiday Favorite Green Beans Almondine 74

Tiramisu 307

Wine suggestion—Cabernet Sauvignon or Shiraz

Passover

Grilled Butterflied Leg of Lamb 163

Chef George's Unbelievable Potato Pancakes 96

The character's of Stew Leonard's help reinforce nutrition tips taught to local elementary school children on Stew's nutrition tours.

Stew's Favorite Grilled
Asparagus 71

Strawberry Crisp 280

Purchased coconut macaroons

Wine suggestion—Dry Riesling
or Sauvignon Blanc

Easter

Georgia Peach Glazed Ham 164

Garlicky-Lemon Roasted
Potatoes 99

Stew's Favorite Grilled
Asparagus 71

Savory Herb-Roasted
Carrots 70

Five-Star Berry Crumb Pie 290

Wine suggestion—Pinot Noir
or Riesling

Simple Everyday Dinner

Easy Italian Chicken Wings 41

Multiple Mushroom Salad 68

Holiday Favorite Green Beans
Almondine 74

The Ultimate Cheeseburger 148

The Stew Leonard's markets
are brightened from spring to
fall with an abundance of shrubs
and flowers in the garden shop.

Tex-Mex Dinner

Caramelized Onion
Quesadillas 38

Sizzling Beef Fajitas 144

Coffee Granita 317

Wine suggestion—Syrah,
Rioja, or Tempranillo

Mother's Day Brunch

Fall Baked French Toast with
Pears and Pecans 332

All-American Fruit Salad 335

Cherry-Citrus Tea Scones 318

Wine suggestion—Champagne,
sparkling wine, or Prosecco

Hearty Brunch

Goat Cheese Scrambled
Eggs 331

Hash Browns 327

Florentine Quiche 329

Purchased whole grain toast
and rolls

Sliced melons

Low Country Corn
Muffins 326

Bethy's Blueberry
Muffins 324

Cherry-Citrus Tea Scones 318

Wine suggestion—Chenin
Blanc

Father's Day

Three-Herb-Crusted Flank
Steak 137

Garlic Mashed Potatoes 95

Creamy Caesar Salad 66

Banana Cake with Fresh
Raspberries 302

Wine suggestion—Cabernet
Franc

The colors of the flag are
bursting from our flower department during July 4th week.

Fourth of July

Southern Spiced Shrimp 226

Boiled Lobsters 262

Purchased coleslaw

Cheesy Chopped Avocado
Salad 60

All-American Fruit Salad 335

Connecticut's Favorite
Chocolate Chip Cookies 294

Purchased ice cream

Wine suggestion—Chardonnay
or Pinot Grigio

Summer's Bounty

Sweet Corn Cakes with Plum Tomato Coulis 28

Pork Chops with Granny Smith Applesauce 168

Fresh Provençal Gratin 80

Farm Fresh Fruit Compote 285

Wine suggestion—Pinot Noir

Labor Day

Beer Can Chicken 191

Mozzarella Caprese Salad 65

Warm Sweet Potato Salad 61

Fresh corn on the cob

Port-Glazed Peaches 283

Wine suggestion—Pinot Grigio

Awards Party or Movie Night

Sweet or Spicy Mixed Nuts 42

Crudités with Mediterranean Dip 34

Fiesta Bowl 85

Coconut Bread Pudding with Dried Apricots 323

Wine suggestion—Sauvignon Blanc

Rosh Hashana

Rosemary Roasted Chicken 200

Savory Herb-Roasted Carrots 70

Warm Sweet Potato Salad 61

Coffee Granita 317

Wine suggestion—Chardonnay

Halloween

Crudités with Mediterranean Dip 34

My Kids' Favorite Mac 'n Cheese 108

Chai Spiced Coffee 316

Al Roker gets into the action making fresh mozzarella cheese during the taping of his show Roker on the Road.

Executive Chef George Llorens cuts one of the thousands of turkeys Stew Leonard's prepares each Thanksgiving.

Thanksgiving

Sweet or Spicy Mixed Nuts 42

Holiday Roast Turkey with Gravy 214

Pears and Pecan Holiday Stuffing 125

Stew Leonard's Rich and Delicious Mashed Potatoes 94

Sesame Sugar Snap Peas 73

Buttery Broccoli with Toasted Pine Nuts 81

French-Style Apple Tarte 288

Port Wine Cake 304

Wine suggestion—Viognier or Pinot Noir

Chanukah

Fruited Chicken 182

Family's traditional latkes

Green salad with Honey-Mustard Vinaigrette 51

Purchased Chanukah cookies

Purchased Chanukah donuts

Wine suggestion—Pinot Grigio or Sauvignon Blanc

Christmas

Herbed Beef Tenderloin with Tawny Port Sauce 138

Vermont Cheddar Mashed Potatoes 95

Buttery Broccoli with Toasted Pine Nuts 81

Purchased dinner rolls

Flourless Chocolate Cake 301

Wine suggestion—Zinfandel

Holiday Dinner

Crudités with Mediterranean Dip 34

Mesclun Salad with Pears and Stilton 55

Vermont Cheddar Cauliflower Gratin 78

Veal Chops Saltimbocca 161

Wine suggestion—Cabernet

Thousands of customers gather for the annual Menorah and Christmas tree lighting.

New Year's Eve Cocktail Party

Sweet or Spicy Mixed Nuts 42

Popular Potato Crisps 37

Blue Ribbon Blue Cheese Coins 32

Crudités with Mediterranean Dip 34

Caramelized Onion Quesadillas 38

Horseradish-Beef Pinwheels 40

Wine suggestion—Merlot or Cabernet

New Year's Eve Dinner Party

Arugula-Endive Salad with Parmesan Crisps 52

Scallops of Veal with Artichoke Hearts 156

Hot cooked fettuccine

Flourless Chocolate Cake 301

Wine suggestion—Pinot Noir

New Year's Day Lunch

Tuscan Pork Roast 167

Sesame Sugar Snap Peas 73

Vermont Cheddar Cauliflower Gratin 78

Green salad with Poppy Seed Dressing 50

Port Wine Cake 304

Wine suggestion—Barbera

INDEX

Note: <u>Underscored</u> page references indicate boxed food tips.
Boldface references indicate photographs.